Uncovering the Secret o

Say No &
Set Boundaries

**How to Take Back Control of Your Life, Embrace
Self-Confidence, Foster Healthy Relationships, and
Cultivate Inner Peace**

MARIA REED

Table of Contents

Introduction

Setting boundaries - a widely discussed and explosive topic. As our times become more modern and fast-paced, our interconnectedness and influences increase, bringing us face-to-face with the importance of personal boundaries. What do personal boundaries mean, and how do they impact our lives? Where do we find them important, and where do conflicts arise? Why is it challenging to establish boundaries, and what do we fear? What could we gain if we confidently and thoughtfully set our boundaries? Embarking on the journey of self-knowledge and exploration can be daunting as we confront secret fears and deep wounds.

Setting boundaries requires the courage to take a stand - recognizing our worth as individuals deserving of protection and having a unique perspective. However, this journey also forces us to confront the wounds that have led us to deny our worth thus far. It prompts us to question our origins, our destination, the company we keep, and how we invest our energy. Exploring boundaries encompasses all of these aspects.

It is a continuous and transformative journey where personal boundaries are ever-shifting and realigning based on our individual growth. Throughout our lives, our boundaries act as a reflection of our personality. At times, we appreciate the clear distinction they provide from an external environment that doesn't align with us. Yet, there are moments when the picture becomes blurred, and our half-formed boundaries bring us pain. Nevertheless, healthy boundaries also bring the pain of separation from the familiar. We outgrow our old boundaries, leaving behind what is known and tested as we embark on the path of self-discovery and reinvention.

Ultimately, healthy and clear boundaries form the foundation for a well-rounded individual who is spiritually, emotionally, and physically sound. With the protection of our personal guardians, we can confidently navigate the world, saying no when necessary and embracing what aligns with our inner convictions.

This book is suitable for you if you...

- Frequently contemplate your true identity and seek to foster the growth of a healthy personality.
- Desire to discover more self-confidence and cultivate a powerful sense of self.
- Wish to strengthen your resilience in conflicts and communicate with greater clarity.
- Want to channel your energy and strength into areas that align with your authentic nature.
- No longer wish to be confined by unfulfilling pursuits.
- Seek to master the art of saying no.
- Strive to improve your self-perception and embark on a journey of self-discovery.
- Desire practical guidance that supports your personal growth.

With this guidebook, you embark on an inner journey that has the potential to bring about significant changes in your life and set you on the path you have long yearned for. It's time to venture into new horizons, to the realm of independence and the unfettered, personal expression of your impact in this world.

Chapter 1

Setting Boundaries – What Does It Mean?

"Without boundaries, everything fades away, including freedom."

Prof. Querulix

In many ways, boundaries serve as markers, divisions, and categorizations of experiences, perspectives, and ways of life. When countries have distinct borders, unique cultures, and everyday spaces emerge, each carrying its own special essence. Similarly, when individuals create boundaries between themselves, they establish personal spaces where they can flourish and engage with others. These boundaries become our homes, our roots, where we feel and experience our individuality, shaping our sense of self. Boundaries not only separate one area from another but also safeguard and appreciate what lies within.

Throughout our lives, we develop different views and perspectives regarding our boundaries:

"My inner self is vulnerable and requires protection."

"The outside world is filled with negativity and must be kept at bay."

"Internal growth takes time and unfolds gradually."

"External influences can overwhelm and overshadow the internal world."

"Strengthening the internal self allows for safe and collaborative interactions with the outside world."

"Although we are interconnected, we still need a framework to anchor ourselves."

"I feel empowered when I establish healthy boundaries to guide me."

"I perceive others as stronger while I feel helpless when my boundaries are crossed."

Your boundaries shape your world and everyday life. They determine the social structures you inhabit, the dynamics of your relationships, your overall well-being, your chosen career path, the atmosphere within your family, and how you navigate your past experiences. Your boundaries encompass your entire life, both internally and externally. When you assert boundaries by saying no, certain elements depart from your life. Conversely, when you say yes, those aspects flourish. When you feel uncertain and fail to take a clear stance, it manifests as chaos and uncertainty in various aspects of your life.

The Individual with Healthy Boundaries

A person who establishes healthy boundaries has developed a solid inner foundation in many aspects. Their beliefs reinforce their self-worth and reflect it to the outside world. Their boundaries convey the message: "I am valuable, I am loved, and I have the autonomy to say yes or no as I please."

Healthy boundaries not only consider the self but also take into account others and the external environment. They prompt questions such as: What happens when I set specific boundaries? What are the consequences for myself and others? How does the situation evolve? Do I desire this outcome, or can I adjust my boundaries differently? Which boundaries are non-negotiable, and which ones am I open to changing?

We can identify a healthy individual by their noticeable presence. Their personality is palpable, enabling us to recognize their values and what matters to them through their charisma. Such individuals are at peace within themselves because they have aligned with their inner truth and established their territory. Their clear boundaries provide concrete indications and guidance regarding appropriate behavior toward them. Moreover, their disposition is one of openness, even when they assert a firm no. They have arranged themselves in their terrain in a way that avoids excessive defensiveness or emotional barriers. They take themselves seriously, know their wants and needs, and prioritize their own boundaries.

Healthy boundaries convey:

- ◆ I can take care of myself.
- ◆ I have a sense of efficacy.
- ◆ I communicate my grievances.
- ◆ If I say yes, you can rely on me.
- ◆ If I say no, I remain true to my feelings.
- ◆ I take responsibility for my decisions.
- ◆ I value myself, and I expect you to value me too.
- ◆ I don't engage in manipulative games.

An individual with healthy boundaries consistently contemplates the balance between connection and autonomy. They make deliberate choices about which beliefs and connections they embrace and which aspects they separate from to follow their own path.

Additionally, exploring healthy boundaries involves honoring one's gut feelings and taking them seriously. Authentic boundaries are not solely based on rational decisions but also on the emotional and physical signals our bodies provide. Our experiences and associated beliefs are stored there, consciously or unconsciously influencing how we navigate our lives.

Those who have internalized healthy boundaries also practice acceptance of what is. They delve into their past, reconcile with their history and its associated boundaries, and appreciate their own perspective as it manifests in the present. Having experienced hurt at some point, they have learned the importance of clearly expressing their boundaries to prevent recurring pain. Such an attitude fosters a sense of self-acceptance and self-love, embracing one's unique biography and innate disposition. Only when we accept ourselves, respecting existing boundaries within our personal history, can we embark on a journey of personal growth, autonomous transformation, and the establishment of new boundaries that support our individual development and inner healing.

An individual with healthy boundaries acknowledges:

- I don't need to justify myself.
- I don't owe anyone anything that doesn't align with my values, and the world doesn't owe me anything.
- I don't have to seek universal approval.
- I don't have to do everything.
- When I say yes to things that are right for me, I have everything I need.
- I actively shape my life and make decisions based on what I want and don't want—I am the protagonist in my own story.

Inspiration

Do you know someone in your environment who you believe excels at setting boundaries? What aspects of their behavior impress you? What valuable lessons can you learn from this person?

Consider engaging in a conversation with them, seeking their insights and experiences to enhance your own growth.

Tip: When seeking to acquire new skills or knowledge, it is beneficial to seek out individuals who have already accomplished what you aspire to achieve. By doing so, you can expand your horizons, educate yourself, gain fresh perspectives, and pursue your goals with valuable support.

The Individual with Insecure or Missing Boundaries

Some individuals feel they lack the right to establish boundaries and create personal space. They frequently experience boundary violations because they are either unaware of their own boundaries or suppress them.

They have internalized beliefs such as:

- I am unworthy of protection.
- My needs are unimportant.
- I must take a back seat.
- I am burdensome and disruptive when I set boundaries and don't comply.
- I am merely a minor character in other people's lives.

These beliefs manifest through withdrawal and silence. They allow themselves to be persuaded to say yes when they mean no in order to avoid displeasing others. They seek to earn love through conformist behavior. Instead of considering their own wants and needs, they prioritize what the other person desires, hoping to gain acceptance and a sense of belonging. Deep down, individuals with insecure boundaries are convinced that they are not loved and undeserving of affection.

In contrast to their own limits, they often unconsciously focus on studying the boundaries of others closely and strive to adhere to them. This behavior is not solely driven by common sense and respect for others but also by a deep-seated fear of being too much. They secretly dread being punished with love withdrawal or losing the relationship. As a result, these individuals constantly assume responsibility within the other person's realm, neglecting their own. A classic example is the office worker who knows the boss's desk better than the boss, takes care of all their tasks, brings them coffee, and even decorates their office with flowers. However, at home, after time, they struggle to create a small space of comfort in their own bed. They invest all their energy into relieving the boss of decision-making, fearing rejection. This behavior disguises underlying fears:

- I am afraid you will reject me if you set your boundaries and turn away.
- I struggle to communicate my boundaries, and perhaps you won't either until it's too late, leading to an explosion.
- I only feel safe if I can interpret your signals myself rather than expecting healthy communication from you.
- I don't even know my own limits, and I fear discovering them because it might require changing my entire life.
- I am afraid of being alone when I set boundaries.

Another clear sign of missing or unsafe boundaries is their exaggerated and forceful expression. Some individuals have been conditioned to be defensive, or they are just beginning to realize the importance of respecting their boundaries. However, this territory is still new to them and may have seemed dangerous due to past experiences. As a result, they tend to assert their boundaries forcefully and loudly. This behavior reflects their insecurity, and their charisma communicates:

- ◆ I feel insecure.
- ◆ I must apologize for my choices.
- ◆ I owe explanations, but I don't want to provide any— just leave me alone!
- ◆ I'm not entirely convinced yet that I'm truly allowed to do this.

Through gruffness, conflict avoidance, or overreactions, they keep others at a distance and create a wide personal space around them, even though they may long for connection and closeness. This is an indication that their boundaries were not taken seriously or were violated in the past. To avoid repeating such experiences, these individuals adhere to an over-protected framework that is so closed off that positive interactions are limited.

Chapter 2
Missing Boundaries – Missing Ego

"When one recognizes their limits very intensely, one must be transformed."

Franz Kafka

I Am My Limits

Identification with one's own boundaries is reflected in the active shaping of everyday life. Orienting yourself to boundaries delineates the terrain in which you navigate. When you are clear about your boundaries, you can confidently say, "This is me. From here to there. Right now, this is my world." With this self-image, you can engage with others, inviting them into your world and revealing aspects of yourself that align with your boundaries.

You are constantly evolving - every day is an opportunity for growth. You undergo changes, learn new things, let go of old ones, reshape your beliefs and perspectives, and make choices that shape the person you will become in the future.

Therefore, your boundaries are not fixed for all time; they are always evolving. However, they can always be clear and distinct, especially when you have a deep understanding of who you are and where you want to grow.

Your boundaries provide you with a sense of identity. That's why it's impactful when they are disregarded, undervalued, or not taken seriously. Such experiences can affect your self-perception and raise the question, "Who am I?" from an uncertain standpoint that echoes negative beliefs, questioning your worth.

You can counteract this by consciously choosing a path and aligning your development in a direction that suits you. You will naturally say no at various points and establish boundaries, asserting, "This behavior, this offer, this relationship is not aligned with my path; it's not beneficial for me. This is a boundary, and I won't compromise it." By doing so, you gain clarity about your journey and your internal goals.

The threads that weave through our lives, encompassing our relationships, vocations, self-image, and worldview, are intertwined with our limitations. They emerge alongside our awareness of our goals. However, it does not mean that we are equally skilled at maintaining and communicating our boundaries. Often, our desires, dreams, and aspirations guide us before we have fully learned to take care of ourselves, resulting in challenges in aligning our behavior accordingly.

We may wonder why our dreams remain unfulfilled, why we continue to experience disrespect in relationships, or why we feel trapped in the never-ending cycle of work - especially when we believed that merely having faith in our dreams would make them come true.

The reason behind this is that our dreams have not yet become an integral part of our identity, and we have not undergone the inner transformation required to establish appropriate boundaries. It involves:

- Wanting a relationship where we are treated lovingly - no longer accepting disrespectful behavior.
- Desiring independence - actively pursuing self-education, taking necessary steps, and refusing to be taken advantage of.
- Aspiring to have a successful relationship with our children as a mother - learning to be present and assertive when needed.
- Wishing for various things and acting accordingly.
- Rejecting interference.
- Seeking kind and respectful communication.

Your emotions play a crucial role in truly connecting with your boundaries and living them. When you authentically feel who you want to be, the transformation begins, empowering you to align your boundaries with your true self. This sense of identification radiates clarity that resonates with others and alleviates the struggle to be seen and understood.

I Feel My Needs Through My Boundaries

Your needs represent your deepest longings that seek fulfillment. Firstly, you desire the satisfaction of your basic needs, which are inherent to every human being. These needs pertain to your physiological well-being: food, water, sleep, sex—essentials that keep your body alive and serve as the foundation for the survival and perpetuation of humanity.

When your basic needs are met, you can then focus on attending to your other needs, ensuring that your spirit, soul, and personality also flourish and thrive.

According to Maslow's hierarchy of needs, the next stage encompasses security. This includes aspects such as housing, work, and income—factors that contribute to a sense of stability. When you have a secure foundation, your brain's stress center can relax, enabling you to concentrate on your personal development, healing, and enjoyment, and align yourself accordingly. The specific manifestations of housing, work, and income may vary depending on the culture, economy, and social environment in which you find yourself. Many individuals are strongly influenced by what appears to be pre-determined, fulfilling their need for security based on learned patterns, often disregarding their personal boundaries without even realizing it.

Example:

Max barely manages to get through his school years, scraping by. He finds little joy in the educational system; the early mornings and the method of learning deeply disgust him. However, being young and lacking sufficient self-reflection, he struggles to identify the specific ways in which his personal boundaries are being violated. Instead, he attempts to distract himself by partying with friends, indulging in alcohol, ultimately resulting in an average academic performance.

Upon leaving school, Max is confronted with the decision of pursuing an apprenticeship within the limited options available based on his academic qualifications. Unable to find a profession that truly captivates him and with an unattainable passion for biology and research, he quickly succumbs to his parents' advice and embarks on carpentry training. "There's always demand for carpenters," his father says. "At least here, you'll have a stable income." Max desires financial security as well, but his discomfort grows with each passing day. The work environment is highly hierarchical, and he frequently finds himself subjected to his boss's whims. However, Max's own negative mood exacerbates the existing misunderstandings and breakdowns in communication on a daily basis.

Thus, another three years pass by, during which Max finds a sense of security through a stable job but endures ongoing emotional suffering and a longing for personal growth. His boundaries are repeatedly crossed because he has not yet developed the ability to take independent responsibility for his emotional well-being and forge his own path. As a result, he experiences constant dissatisfaction. Saying no at this point to the path he has been following thus far would greatly benefit him in aligning with his true desire to pursue something that truly resonates with him. By setting boundaries that guide him in the right direction, he can channel his energy towards balancing the need for security with personal development. This can only be achieved by freeing himself from the expectations of others and allowing himself to discover his own path.

Currently, Max still defines his identity by functioning and conforming to the basics of his life. Moreover, his identification with the third set of needs in Maslow's hierarchy plays a significant role: social needs. We all possess a strong need for belongingness. Partnerships, friendships, and family form a crucial foundation for our emotional well-being. Max secretly fears losing this support network if he deviates from his parents' advice and follows his own path. His limit in this area is deeply buried within his adherence to others' expectations. In order to maintain his place in the community, he compromises his own boundaries and acquiesces to his parents' wishes, despite their disapproval of his desire to pursue a higher education diploma and a degree in biology. In his professional development, Max constantly feels that the limits within which he operates are externally imposed on him: his bank account, parents, teachers, and boss dictate his path. He does not establish boundaries independently from within, resulting in frequent clashes with the prevailing system in his life. Emotionally, this takes a toll on his well-being, and at the age of 26, Max finds himself trapped in a persistent state of depression.

I Lose Sight of Myself When I'm Unaware of My Limits

During this period, Max experiences a profound sense of disconnection from himself. He finds himself asking the same questions repeatedly:

- Who am I?
- What do I truly want, and why am I not achieving it?
- What can I accept and what are my non-negotiable boundaries?
- If I were to make decisions for myself, where would I say yes and where would I say no? What truly matters to me?

For the first time, Max consciously realizes that he cannot continue on this path. He needs to assert himself. He needs to determine how he will fulfill his basic needs and longing for belonging within the boundaries he sets for himself. He reflects on the people he wants to spend time with, those who will support and encourage him on his journey. He has conversations with his parents, making it clear that he will now make different choices than what had been expected of him. Initially, setting this boundary challenges his need for belongingness, as his parents do not respond enthusiastically. However, Max is in the midst of a process of shifting and redefining his boundaries. In the long run, he prioritizes maintaining his social connections. If he were to persist in allowing others to dictate his path, his boundaries would continually be violated, becoming more evident as his personality develops. He would progressively lose himself in the desire to please others and relinquish control over setting his own limits. Ultimately, this would lead to a sense of not living his own life, but rather being a pawn in the lives of others.

I Do Not Live My Life If I Do Not Live My Limits

Another example:

Marjorie finds herself in the same situation over and over again: no sooner has she found a new partner than she feels herself merging into the relationship. All her ambitions, goals, ideas, productivity, and sense of purpose seem to fade away. Instead, in a short period of time, she aligns all her plans with her partner's schedule and preferences, regardless of whether he expects it or not. It appears that she carries within her a pattern of conformity that hinders her from maintaining her boundaries when in the presence of a loved one.

Initially, the relationship is very harmonious because Marjorie adapts strongly, resulting in minimal conflicts. However, after a few weeks, her partner visibly becomes strained, almost annoyed. He cannot comprehend what is happening in Marjorie's mind and why she does not assert her own clear viewpoints. He desires a tangible counterpart who actively contributes to shaping their daily life, engages in discourse, and is not afraid of healthy opposition.

Instead, he gets the impression that Marjorie is increasingly becoming a mere extension of himself. Marjorie herself also suffers from this internal pattern, as she goes to great lengths to be loved and accepted by conforming, yet seemingly achieves the opposite. Over time, her partner becomes more distant, eventually leading to the breakdown of the relationship.

Throughout these experiences, Marjorie feels disconnected from herself and struggles to cultivate a life beyond the inner compulsion to please her partner and remain close to him. Her longing for intimacy overshadows her need for autonomy.

Marjorie, therefore, ponders:

- What am I afraid of experiencing when I establish boundaries that allow my true personality to shine?
- What do I long for the most?
- What causes me to remain silent, neglect my own needs, and even feel a strong desire to become a dependent attachment?

- How is it possible that I feel vibrant and alive when I am alone, but all of this dissipates once I enter into a relationship?
- Why do I believe that I can only live within my limits if no one challenges them?

Another example:

For Sabrina, the dynamics of her romantic life are quite the opposite: she yearns deeply for closeness and intimacy but feels the need to fiercely defend her boundaries. She often initiates conflicts out of fear of not being seen or respected or when it comes to reaching a compromise.

Sabrina frequently implies that her partner fails to appreciate her boundaries, despite his sincere efforts to make her feel secure.

In her own words, "Whenever I have to make compromises, it feels like I'm losing my sense of self, betraying myself, and no longer living within my own authenticity. I feel constrained and depleted."

On the other hand, there exists an immense longing within Sabrina for love, connection, and an equal partnership. She wrestles with the challenge of revealing more of herself to her partner and allowing him to deeply touch her heart. This process of living with boundaries also entails opening them in the right places and inviting loved ones into her inner realm.

For Sabrina, trust is the key tool that enables this process. Without trust, it becomes difficult to open her boundaries and share them with her partner in a way that allows for the co-creation of an interpersonal space. When the trust she extends is accepted, appreciated, and valued, Sabrina's boundaries remain intact and are not forcefully crossed by her partner. She invites him to honor and incorporate her boundaries into their shared space, and she allows him to take personal responsibility for maintaining those boundaries. In this way, she no longer needs to vigilantly guard herself, constantly on the lookout for any potential violation or infringement. She knows that in this space, she can let go and trustingly share the responsibility for nurturing a successful relationship with her partner.

Both Marjorie and Sabrina share a common desire for a fulfilling relationship that enriches their overall lives. Living their lives, for both of them, involves realizing this dream and cultivating vibrant connections. To do so, they must come to terms with their limitations and learn how to authentically express them. Neither abandoning their boundaries nor fiercely defending them will bring them closer to their goal. The ability to truly know and value oneself is essential for the possibility of an authentic and mutually fulfilling relationship built on equality and shared understanding.

Inspiration

Imagine a garden that serves as a symbolic representation of your inner being, your soul, your life, and your essence. Envision this garden painted in colors that resonate with you, and visualize the various areas within it taking the form of plants that are both precious and harmoniously come together to create a beautiful garden picture. However, also allow the flowers and plants that evoke conflicting emotions or require more care and attention to appear in your mind's eye.

Now, observe closely: Notice that the garden is enclosed by a fence. Take a moment to examine the fence and consider its composition. What material is it made of? Is it adorned with any decorations? Is it tall or low, giving off a sense of coldness? Can you see through it, or is it opaque? Envision the fence as a representation of your boundaries.

Next, visualize a door, a small gate within the fence. How does this gate appear to you? Is it locked, or is it open? Who holds the key to this gate? Is it solely in your possession, or do others have access as well?

This inner imagery should align with your current feelings and perception of your life, your inner self, and your limits. By doing this exercise, you can gain insight into the state of your boundaries and gain clarity on any changes or desires you may have.

The imagery of the inner garden offers valuable insights into how much you are truly living your own life at this moment and indicates areas where you may lack confidence as well as the level of self-worth you hold.

The Garden

The garden serves as a symbolic representation of what is significant to you—your soul, your emotions, your sense of self. It paints a unique image that reflects who you are. Do you find contentment in what you see? Which areas require your attention? Is there a tree striving to grow beyond the confines of the fence? What does it signify? Where do you yearn for expansion and personal growth? Are there plants in your garden that you do not desire? Do they overshadow other plants, depriving them of light and water? Which section of the garden appears particularly beautiful, resonating with your aspirations and happiness? Do you feel a sense of ownership over this garden—does it embody your true essence? Or does it seem burdened by elements that weigh you down more than they bring you joy?

Components within your garden may encompass:

- Relationships (feel free to specify individuals)
- Engagements and commitments
- Goals and dreams
- Current occupation
- Abilities and character traits
- Emotions and sentiments
- Needs and desires

The Fence

Encircling your unique garden are the boundaries—the fence. The characteristics and construction of the fence reveal insights into your self-relationship and the manner in which you navigate your boundaries. What do the fence's material and structure signify to you? Does wood denote an affinity for your emotions and empathetic attentiveness to your needs? Does rigid metal imply closure and detachment or even a sense of helplessness? What do any gaps between the fence slats represent? How deeply are you willing to let others see, and how deeply do you desire to be seen? Are there any holes in the fence that you have long wished to mend? What currently flows through them? Do you desire to retain it within your garden? Is it causing harm to any elements within? Does the light you have yearned for seep through the cracks, nourishing your plants?

The fence provides insights into:

- Your affirmations and negations
- Your uncertainties
- Your clarity
- Your volition
- Your hopes
- Your orientation
- Your stance toward the external world and your internal garden

The garden and its surrounding fence aim to reveal how you perceive and experience your boundaries in the present moment, shedding light on the overall impression they leave upon you.

And Me?

You are the gardener—the caretaker. You are entrusted with the responsibility of tending to your garden, protecting it, and fostering a magnificent ecosystem that harmonizes with the outside world in the appropriate places. You have the freedom to choose which plants thrive here, cultivate the soil, and provide shade, water, and light as needed. You can allow entry and invite departure, caution unsuspecting visitors, and establish guidelines for being in your garden. You have the agency to shape it according to your preferences—for your well-being, healing, and personal growth. If the inner image reveals that someone else holds the key to your garden, you can address that and reclaim control. You can also choose to collaborate with others, allowing them to contribute their own plants. Alternatively, you may prefer to have guests rather than permanent residents. How do you wish to interact with the outside world?

These boundaries are yours, deserving of protection. By assuming the role of guardian and taking responsibility for what transpires within, you truly live your life.

Chapter 3

The Conflict with One's Own Boundaries

"Limitations always make for happiness."

Arthur Schopenhauer

It could be so simple, couldn't it? Boundaries provide security, as we learned in fortunate circumstances during childhood. Our parents and guardians created a framework within which we could operate. Today, we navigate different boundaries that surround us: the political landscape, the laws of the land, and our social and community environment. These external boundaries give us a certain direction, and if we feel comfortable within them, they offer security by limiting our choices to a manageable level.

However, over the years, internal limits have also formed within us—boundaries that are shaped by our personality and experiences. Just like the saying goes, "A leopard can't change its spots." Our personality carries a unique imprint that restricts our choices in certain areas. Changing deeply ingrained aspects of our personality requires profound transformation, unwavering determination, and a specific goal, or else we will revert back to our habitual patterns of behavior and thinking. It is important to differentiate between our inherent personality and learned or conditioned behaviors. Embracing the inner boundaries of our core personality allows us to stay true to ourselves and further develop into the person we already are at our core. Conversely, striving to become someone fundamentally different leads to a deep fragmentation of our own soul.

Boundaries offer security and guidance, but it is essential to discern which boundaries truly support us and which ones hinder our growth. It can be challenging to navigate the dense jungle of our emotions, as our feelings are strongly influenced by past experiences and behavioral patterns. Sometimes, a boundary may even feel comforting because we are accustomed to it, but upon closer examination, it reveals itself as a façade. How can we begin to unravel this tangled web and identify the starting point of the red thread? What should we be mindful of?

To understand this, it is worthwhile to reflect on the past:

Powerlessness: When Others Defined My Boundaries

Powerlessness is a constant companion for many children during their early years. They have wants, desires, longings, and dreams, but it is the parents who make the decisions and take the lead. The child, not yet capable of understanding many connections, often finds their needs ignored because the parents are unable to align with the child's perspective and empathize with them for various reasons. Powerlessness emerges when one's voice goes unheard when one is unseen, dismissed, and not taken seriously. It whispers, "I surrender. There is nothing I can do here. I feel trapped. I am frightened. I am powerless and ineffective."

For many people, this deeply ingrained sense of powerlessness persists into adulthood. We yearn to seize control of our lives, to establish our own boundaries, and to become the guardians of our own destinies. Yet, we have experienced a lack of trust in our ability to do so, and we have allowed others to take charge and make decisions that shape our entire existence. Consequently, even as adults, we often feel powerless and impotent, despite having the right and even the responsibility to carve out our own place in this world. We find ourselves seeking external boundaries and conforming to directional signs that provide us with a sense of orientation. We struggle to let go of our powerlessness and take full control of the steering wheel.

Powerlessness arises not only from the inappropriate relinquishment of responsibility but also from the violation of our personal boundaries. Those who have experienced assault, whether physical, emotional, or spiritual, often carry deep wounds that speak volumes: others dictate my life. They have authority over my most private matters, over everything that is sacred to me. I am weak and helpless, unable to take action.

The experience of weakness can trigger an underlying terror that may not be readily apparent. Many people lead seemingly normal lives, going to work every day, taking care of their children, and fulfilling their duties. Yet, deep within, there is a hidden feeling that whispers: I am incapable of handling all of this. I have no clue how to navigate any of it. I cannot truly tap into my own potential for productivity and creativity. I am feeble, replaceable. The truly significant decisions are always made by others.

Example:

Ben's mother exerted control over him at every turn. Driven by fear that he couldn't gauge his own limits and needed constant guidance, she supported him in everything, well beyond the appropriate age and even in tasks he had already mastered. She seemed oblivious to his development and competencies, leaving Ben with the belief that he couldn't truly accomplish anything on his own and that he wasn't trusted. Frustrated and lacking the will to assert himself, he eventually surrendered, allowing his mother to shape his everyday life and succumbing to her control.

As an adult, this experience of powerlessness carried over into his relationships with close caregivers. He sought out partners who exhibited controlling behavior, relinquishing control over daily matters and displaying passive-aggressive tendencies. Furthermore, his friends often felt that Ben lacked a personal opinion or firm stance on various topics. He would often shrug his shoulders or change his mind depending on who he was talking to. A friend once remarked, "It always felt like you were swayed by external influences. People couldn't engage with you on an equal footing."

Fear: When Others Crossed My Boundaries

Crossing boundaries, as mentioned before, not only triggers powerlessness but also fear. This fear often leads to three primary reaction patterns: fight, flight, or freeze. Fear sends us a signal: "It's dangerous here, it's not safe, something can harm us." In response, we instinctively engage in immediate action for self-preservation, setting aside logical thinking. Fear compels us to fight off anything that appears threatening, to flee when our boundaries are violated, or to freeze, allowing ourselves to be overwhelmed and subjected to repeated experiences that deepen our pain and fear.

When your boundaries are crossed, evoking fear, you have developed individual behavioral responses within the pattern of fight-flight-freeze. As a child, you employed survival strategies dictated by fear. It is important to remember that fear itself is not the problem. It aims to protect you. When you feel fear, there is a reason behind it. It may indicate real danger or remind you of a past negative experience. Fear can also arise from imagined future scenarios, often influenced by a worldview shaped by your past experiences: "It's not safe here."

Common protective mechanisms include:

- Attack: tantrums, accusations, physical aggression, insults, devaluation, active resistance in various forms...
- Flight: leaving the room, remaining silent, turning away, shrinking oneself, relinquishing responsibility...
- Freeze: silence, conflict avoidance, dissociation...

Fear compels us to safeguard our core, but it also robs us of control. We become driven by the fear of losing something vital for our survival, relinquishing our ability to master our own senses.

Example:

Lydia, now in her forties, still bears the trauma of being regularly beaten as a child. This trauma heavily influences her relationship with her husband. Whenever she harbors a differing opinion secretly, it takes her minutes to gather the courage to express it, as her cellular system fears the punishment that may follow. In conflicts with her husband, she quickly falls silent and gives up. She often finds herself doing things she doesn't want to do, obediently following her husband's dictates, even though he doesn't demand obedience. Growing up, Lydia learned from her parents that her needs ranked lowest within the family and were disregarded in planning and decision-making. Any sign of rebellion was met with punishment. Consequently, Lydia internalized the belief that her boundaries and needs held no significance in interpersonal relationships and that standing up for them would only invite punishment.

Fear runs deep as the experiences that trigger it become ingrained in our nervous system. Simply being aware of what has happened may not be enough. Seeking help to process the emotional impact of these experiences can be beneficial. Working through the underlying triggers allows for the learning of new behaviors. While the following tools can offer assistance in specific situations, for deeper traumas, it is advisable to consult an appropriate expert:

- ◆ Counting and breathing: Close your eyes, count to ten, and focus on calm, deep breathing.

- ◆ In moments of panic: Sit with your back against a wall, without a chair, engaging your legs to ground yourself in your body while maintaining calm, deep breaths.

- ◆ Find humor: Concentrate on a lighthearted moment and laugh. The brain cannot simultaneously experience fear and laughter.

- ◆ In a trusting relationship, communicate your anxiety, preferably during non-acute moments. Explain to your partner what you need from them when you're feeling anxious.

Shame: When Others Ignored and Ridiculed My Boundaries

When boundaries are ignored or dismissed, the impact can be just as painful as when boundaries are violated or disregarded out of a need for connection. Every outward expression of longing, every invitation to be seen and acknowledged, every plea from a child saying, "Look at me! Look at me!" represents a boundary either put on display to attract attention or a gate that is opened to let someone come closer.

Shame arises when a person exposes their deepest inner self and is met with a lack of recognition or dismissal of their offering. It is in those moments where individuals truly reveal themselves and present their being that they also expose their limits to the outside world, asking, "Do you love me as I am? With my nos and yeses, with my clear or unclear boundaries, with my certainties and insecurities?"

This vulnerability is an attempt to create genuine intimacy, to be seen and acknowledged.

After experiencing shame, many children unconsciously decide to no longer reveal their authentic selves but instead play a role. They closely observe which behaviors are recognized and rewarded in their environment, particularly by individuals who display certain behaviors (such as siblings or friends with their parents), in order to achieve the desired effect. These adapted roles include:

- Earning kindness through being good
- Receiving praise through performance
- Later in life, seeking physical attention through presenting oneself in a proper manner
- Seeking attention by presenting content that interests the listener
- ...

By adopting these roles, the child assumes a persona that does not truly align with their inner self. They prioritize survival, remaining within the group, and securing the attention of their caregivers, even if it means sacrificing their authenticity in the worst case.

Deep inside, a profound wound remains: "I am ashamed of who I truly am."

This leads to numerous limiting beliefs that strongly influence later relationships:

- "I am not worthy of your love."
- "You don't want me as I am."
- "I exist to please you, not myself."
- "If I reveal myself, it will cause pain."
- "I hide my most precious aspects to protect them."

These beliefs leave individuals feeling unable to genuinely connect with their loved ones and experiencing loneliness even within relationships.

Example:

At the age of nine, Maya discovered the power of beauty and elegance on others, playing and expressing herself unconsciously. She began dressing creatively and beautifully, openly showcasing her grace and comfort in her own body and being. She never questioned whether she was lovable, interesting enough, or capable of capturing attention when she desired it.

After moving to a new village, Maya encountered new children at the playground, including some boys from a higher grade. She enjoyed playing with them and relished their company.

One day, Maya's mother gave her a new pair of pants, which she proudly wore to share her joy with her new friends. She believed she looked modern, fashionable, and presentable, filled with excitement and energy.

Upon arriving at the playground, she hopped off her bike in a childishly gallant manner and eagerly joined the waiting group. One boy, whom she unconsciously wanted to impress, looked her up and down and dryly remarked, "Where did you get that rag?"

At that moment, Maya's heart shattered into a thousand pieces. Her cheeks burned, and she longed for the ground to swallow her whole. At that young age, Maya lacked the ability to respond to the boy's comment with self-assurance, asserting, "I find myself and what I wear beautiful - I stand by myself." Instead, she stood frozen and deeply ashamed in front of the group, unable to move, while the others moved on to other topics, paying her no further attention. When she felt unnoticed, Maya slinked back to her bike and rode home, feeling depressed and profoundly sad.

This kind of pain from shaming and rejection is too overwhelming for many children to bear, causing them to compartmentalize the experience and associated feelings, often suppressing the memory for a long time. However, the consequences of this deep hurt continue to manifest for many years.

Maya forgot the joy of fashion, of proudly presenting herself, and the naturalness of expressing affection. She retreated behind gray shades, becoming quieter and losing her previously loud, cheerful, and vibrant demeanor. In adulthood, before every date, she grappled with the feeling of appearing overdressed or talking too much, fearing being perceived as extravagant and taking up too much space.

Loneliness: When Others Misunderstood My Boundaries

When children express their boundaries, either directly or indirectly, and those boundaries are not understood, it can quickly lead to feelings of exclusion. They struggle to communicate and be understood through words or their behavior, yearning to be seen, but instead experiencing their boundaries being taken personally by others or handled differently than what the child needs in that moment.

The lack of empathy towards our boundaries makes us feel different from others, like an outsider, deviating from what is understood and comprehended by those around us. Moreover, we can feel ashamed for hurting others with our boundaries and being faced with the choice between staying true to ourselves and successfully interacting with others. When a person clarifies their boundary, it is not about the other person but about themselves. They need to experience the other person turning towards them, listening, and responding with understanding and respect. If, on the other hand, the other person is offended by the boundary being set, takes it personally, and only thinks of themselves without showing empathy, the connection that the boundary is meant to establish does not occur. Many boundaries are set to convey the message, "This is me, this is what I don't want, here I say no. But if you can accept me in this way and are willing to do so, a relationship between us is possible and desired."

A boundary is not always a defense but can also be seen as an invitation to meet and truly show each other as we are. This needs to be recognized and appreciated by the other person.

Example:

Lara was always a child who didn't enjoy intense and close physical affection very much. She loved talking, playing, having fun together, singing, dancing, and sharing meals, but physical contact often overwhelmed her, and she quickly reached her limits. In a childlike manner, she would reject her parents' attempts for physical closeness. However, her parents couldn't properly interpret this rejection and felt they had done something wrong, that their daughter didn't love them, or that they needed to reach out to her even more. Often, Lara felt emotionally trapped in this dynamic and didn't know how to help herself. Her parents reacted with offense and resentment, eventually withdrawing out of helplessness, and even their shared activities took on a somber tone. Lara found herself sinking into increasing loneliness. How could she make it clear at such a young age that it was only the physical touch that overwhelmed her? How could she explain that it wasn't a personal dislike for her parents or their desire for connection?

In adulthood, this wound manifested as extreme tension during physical encounters, making it difficult for Lara to let go. She felt lonely in relationships because she consistently sought out partners who placed great importance on physical closeness and reacted defensively when she withdrew. As a result, they engaged in fewer enjoyable activities together that could have helped Lara feel alive and loved in the relationship. Relationships quickly deteriorated, and Lara seemed to find solace in living alone because the constant conflicts, offended reactions, and judgmental looks hurt her more than being in a relationship. She had many casual friendships, but she couldn't find depth in them. It was only through therapy that Lara discovered the deep hurt and loneliness she experienced and its origins. She learned to share and clearly communicate her boundaries while also explaining them in a way that others could better understand her.

Inspiration

Writing Exercise

Imagine fear, shame, powerlessness, and loneliness as colorful little characters inside of you. Write down their appearances, behaviors, and if you like, give them names.

Now, envision yourself sitting at a table with them. Take a moment to write down questions for each of them individually. Ask them how they entered your life, what they protect within you, and why they are still present. Also, inquire about their desires and longings. Let each character express what comes to mind.

Then, it's your turn to speak. You can address all of them collectively or have individual conversations with each character. Share how you would like to live, how you wish to interact with them, and whether you consider ending your collaboration with any of them.

If you wish, you can invite other helpers to the table and propose collaboration.

Example:

Loneliness now collaborates with courage: Despite feeling lonely, I gather all the courage within me to show up and actively seek connection.

Powerlessness teams up with grief and anger: I acknowledge painful situations and allow myself to experience the power of anger and the solace of embracing grief. Anger will empower me to break free from the grip of powerlessness and bring about change.

Shame requires empathy and warmth: I find solace by curling up in bed, covering myself with a cozy blanket, and indulging in a warm cup of tea. I reach out to a friend, make a phone call, or arrange a meeting to open up and share my feelings. The empathetic listener offers understanding and encouragement, providing a different perspective on my experiences and reminding me of my strengths.

Chapter 4

Assessing the Present and Shaping the Future

"It seems to be inherent to human nature that they do not want to admit their boundaries."

Ernst R. Hauschka

The decisions, feelings, actions, patterns, and beliefs we embody today shape the trajectory of our tomorrow and influence the direction we take in life. It is, therefore, crucial to take a moment to assess ourselves, examine our path, and determine where we are headed. A clear sense of direction is essential, as it allows us to navigate the right path and steer ourselves towards our desired destination.

To find a path that aligns with our goals and aspirations, it is valuable to acknowledge and honor our boundaries. Boundaries serve as guideposts, leading us toward our potential and away from what does not resonate with our true selves. Saying a resounding "yes" to what truly matters to us also implies saying "no" to what contradicts our values. It is through this process that our unique path emerges as we navigate through life.

There are limits that stem from our experiences, temperament, and character, shaped by our personal history. Simultaneously, there are limits that point us toward our future, aligning with our desire to grow and evolve in specific directions. By acknowledging the limits that have formed as a result of past experiences, we can approach our full potential with self-love and self-acceptance.

Along our journey, we may encounter limits that initially seem to contradict our ambitions. For instance, we might dislike large crowds but aspire to become a renowned speaker. We might be hesitant to open up about our inner selves while yearning for deep intimacy and meaningful relationships. We might find repetitive daily routines uninspiring but struggle to let go of our attachment to our hometown. We might even experience daily frustration with a loved one yet continue to maintain contact with them.

The limits shaped by our history and the aspirations we hold for the future can merge harmoniously, leading to inner healing, reconciliation, and the conscious shaping of our own path with responsibility and self-empowerment. In this journey, it is beneficial to reflect on our current state in relation to our inner longings. Below, you will find areas that can serve as mirrors for self-reflection.

I Struggle to Say No - A Yearning for Confidence

Examples:

- *Melanie's desk is overflowing with files, and as soon as she completes one task, another one lands on her plate. Her overtime hours keep piling up, yet she hasn't received a raise. Her boss claims she lacks the necessary qualifications. Despite this, she is entrusted with delicate customer interactions—everyone recognizes her meticulous and flawless work and feels assured when she handles their requests. However, gratitude from her superiors remains elusive.*

- *Sasha vividly recalls a childhood incident. She always longed for a best friend. During her elementary school days, she would often stand alone in the schoolyard, watching other children play, never being asked to join in. Finally, a few years later, she befriended the girl next door. This new friend frequently spoke of her previous best friend and confided in Sasha about their fallout due to disagreements. Although it hurt Sasha's heart that her new friend didn't seem as content with their friendship as she had been with the previous one, Sasha remained compassionate and patient. She tried her best to please her friend Laura, molding herself to fit Laura's preferences in both inner and outer aspects. From dress style to developing new interests in the opposite sex, despite not feeling ready herself, to sympathies or aversions towards other children or teachers, and even music preferences—Sasha adjusted everything to align with Laura's guidance, hoping to gain popularity.*

One day, Laura said to her, "I hung out with Anna yesterday, and we made up! Now she's my best friend again. I hope you don't mind. We can still play together." A sharp pain pierced Sasha's heart, and she struggled to hold back her tears. Silently, she nodded while a profound sadness enveloped her soul. She withdrew into herself, spending the rest of the day with Laura, barely uttering a word, desperately clinging to their connection. But her long-held belief had been affirmed: No one truly wants her just as she is.

♦ *Mollie has ventured into entrepreneurship and opened her own tax office. Her friends and family are thrilled to have someone to handle their tax returns. Due to their personal relationship, they expect a substantial discount almost as a given. Mollie, wanting to bring joy to her loved ones, agrees. However, she gradually begins to feel burdened by being taken advantage of. Her livelihood depends on her work, yet she feels undervalued. She wonders, "How can those closest to me expect me to do them a favor that could potentially jeopardize my own well-being, considering the time, energy, and money involved?"*

♦ *Lars is an exceptionally attractive man, well aware of his looks. Countless women are vying for his attention. Deep down, though, Lars feels unloved for who he truly is beyond his physical appearance. He engages in numerous relationships but experiences a profound sense of loneliness and a lack of genuine connection that he yearns for.*

One day, he meets a woman who sees beyond his exterior. She desires a deeper bond with him, but Lars, accustomed to being reduced to his appearance, struggles to accept her affection. Perhaps he senses that a different experience awaits him, yet his lack of self-worth prevents him from embracing it. Instead, he initiates a heated argument and pushes the new girlfriend away. Lars finds himself entangled in countless affairs, constantly feeling used but unable to draw a line and break free from his old patterns.

In hindsight, Lars recalls a pivotal experience from his youth. At a party when he was 15 years old, a classmate said to him, "If you weren't so good-looking, I would have never noticed you. You always sit alone in the back corner and bite on your pen—it's a little strange." Although the remark seemed casual, it inflicted deep pain on Lars. Subconsciously, he resolved to seek attention through superficial connections, despite consistently violating his own boundaries. He yearns for genuine encounters and to be valued beyond his physical appearance.

Many individuals who struggle with setting boundaries often find it difficult to say no. When faced with demands or requests, they quickly respond with a yes and automatically prioritize fulfilling the other person's wishes, disregarding their own desires in the process.

The underlying pain behind this inability to say no often stems from childhood experiences discussed earlier. When our boundaries are disregarded or violated due to ignorance, transgressions, misunderstandings, or control, we develop the belief that we are unworthy of attention, love, and respect. As children, many of us learned that the only way to receive attention from caregivers was through obedience or excessively conforming and subservient behavior. By pleasing others, we earned praise, recognition, brief moments of affection, or even just a smile. This shaped us into so-called people pleasers.

A people pleaser, someone who constantly seeks to please others, instinctively prioritizes whether the other person approves of their actions rather than considering what is genuinely good for themselves. Their own needs for self-acceptance, personal growth, and development take a back seat. The primary focus for a people pleaser is maintaining the relationship with the other person by making themselves indispensable in their lives. They believe that by doing enough for the other person, they can ensure that the relationship remains intact. However, even if this strategy appears to work for a while, it does not fulfill the deep longing for unconditional love within every individual.

Example:

> *Samuel, the third child in a busy family, was considered a latecomer. With an age gap of eight years between him and his two siblings, his parents were reluctant to give up their newfound lifestyle focused on work and external responsibilities rather than prioritizing their children's needs.*
>
> *The limited time the family spent together proved quite challenging for Samuel. His siblings kept themselves occupied, and his parents engaged in what they referred to as "adult conversations." In an attempt to seek attention, Samuel would set up a nice coffee table for the family, draw pictures, tidy up the surroundings, and use facial expressions and gestures to show*

his support and affirmation for the interpersonal interactions in the room. Unfortunately, he only received attention from his siblings when they assigned him household chores, saying things like, "Get me this" or "Do that." The acknowledgment he sought was merely transactional and fleeting.

As Samuel grew into a young adult, he became the designated follower in his social circle—the friend who unquestioningly went along with everything. He offered assistance whenever he sensed a need, tirelessly supporting his friends during their various endeavors, including academic pursuits. Although he possessed many talents and was valued for his expertise by his friends, he received little recognition for his authentic self—his desires, needs, and individuality. Samuel himself struggled to articulate what truly defined him.

At some point, however, Samuel abruptly vanished from the scene without a word, a goodbye, or an explanation. His sudden disappearance left everyone puzzled, and conversations among the group revolved around his absence. They wondered, "He was actually quite nice. Where did he go? How could he leave without informing anyone?"

It was only in Samuel's absence that he was truly noticed. He had been praised for his actions but not for his genuine identity. Only when he vanished did his friends suspect that Samuel was also an individual who desired to be seen and acknowledged. In their discussions with one another, they observed, "He seemed different lately, don't you think? He appeared moody and disinterested as if he was going along with everything without truly wanting to."

Sometimes, there comes a point when the people pleaser reaches a breaking point. Despite their old strategies still working and their continued compliance with deep internal patterns, they begin to experience dissatisfaction, sadness, and anger within themselves. They start to awaken and realize that they actually desire relationships based on equality, where they are loved without having to constantly pay attention.

As the old system gradually collapses, it becomes increasingly challenging to sustain the established structures. The longing for genuine attention and love intensifies, but the question of self-worth remains unanswered due to the absence of corresponding experiences. Consequently, the yes-man expends significant amounts of energy to uphold their role in relationships, yet internally they become restless, irritable, and resentful. Occasionally, these emotions erupt, leaving onlookers puzzled as they struggle to understand the sudden change in the otherwise loving and submissive person. They may secretly wish for the other person to continue fulfilling the unspoken agreement of always saying yes and serving, as both individuals are entwined in their own inner patterns and wounds.

In Samuel's case, a limit became apparent at some point. However, due to his perceived lack of self-worth, he could only express it through a decisive break and a fresh start. Fearful of being hurt and rejected by revealing his true feelings, he did not dare to communicate with his friends and break the pattern. Thus, fleeing seemed to be the only viable option for him because continuing as before was no longer possible.

Now Samuel faces the task of confronting his wounds and engaging in self-reflection. To establish relationships based on equality in the future, it is crucial for him to come to terms with his past and recognize that he now has the capacity to act differently from his childhood survival strategy. By following his longing, Samuel can discover the right path. He is allowed to explore his true desires and focus solely on himself. Initially, he must get to know himself independently of his previous role as a yes-man.

Self-awareness marks the beginning of self-acceptance—a resounding yes to who you are and what you represent. As you become more self-aware of your beliefs and experiences, you gradually realize, "I have a tendency to please everyone, struggle with saying no because I feel unlovable. These beliefs stem from past experiences. However, as an adult, I have the opportunity to create new experiences. I acknowledge that everything I have gone through so far is part of my personal narrative. I am determined to rewrite that story and embrace a different role. I long for self-awareness and for prioritizing my needs, longings, and desires. I want to live, act, and exist in my own power, energy, and worldview. I am no longer a supporting character in other people's lives. I am claiming my rightful place."

Inspiration

Write:

- If everything were possible, I would...
- If I could send someone to the devil, I would...
- Most of all, I would like to stop constantly...
- If I say no at this point, I'm afraid... However, the best thing that could happen would be...
- I imagine my ideal circle of friends like this:...
- I'm going to stop as of today...
- I would like to invest my time more in...

In addition, create a mind map with a big "NO" in the middle. Around this "NO," write down everything to which you want to say no from today onwards. There is also room for areas in which you do not yet feel strong enough to really implement the "NO." By writing them down, your "NO" will become stronger, and you will gain more confidence. Writing them down will breathe life into your "NO" and make it more powerful.

I Am Influenced by Others - I Yearn for Competence

Examples:

- *"I've reached my limit!" exclaims Clarissa, but her voice remains silent. Tension has been building within the team ever since the startup started moving in a direction that Clarissa can no longer ethically support. She was the one who initially came up with the idea, but as the business grew, she brought in employees to assist her. However, things have veered off from Clarissa's original vision. Helplessly, she watches as others take control, unable to assert her position effectively. "Why am I unable to speak up? Why does everything inside me scream, yet I remain silent? Why am I allowing my dream to be taken away without putting up a fight?" She feels that her lack of expertise renders her voiceless, despite being the one who initiated everything.*

- *Miles has been actively involved in a religious community for as long as he can remember. The rules and beliefs provided him with a sense of security, and he followed them out of a deep inner connection. However, as the group evolves into a more rigid and exclusive direction, doubts begin to surface within him. Is what's happening still right? Do I truly believe in it? Is this the life I want to lead? Yet, he hesitates to fully explore these thoughts, as deviating from the religious path could result in social exclusion. Moreover, Miles has been conditioned to believe that teachers and leaders know best and that he should simply follow their guidance. Secretly, he longs to make his own decisions, but he carries a deep sense of guilt and lacks self-trust.*

- *Philipp, a manager in a gym, has been rewarded by his boss with respect and trust for his work. However, when his boss learns of Philipp's plan to start his own business, his attitude changes. He incessantly mentions that Philipp has likely reached his peak position and would struggle to succeed in the free market on his own. Philipp still lacks certain certifications and further training, which he hasn't been able to pursue due to his heavy workload. As a result, he fears that his boss might be right and that staying in a secure job would be a better choice.*

♦ *Melanie's dream to become a coach is big. Every day, she immerses herself in podcasts, videos, books, and courses on relevant topics. She admires established coaches and consultants, aiming to be like them. However, something doesn't quite resonate with the system. She often finds herself thinking that there are aspects she would like to approach differently. She doesn't want to rely solely on the internet, engage in extensive advertising, or constantly put herself in the spotlight. Deep inside, a voice whispers that there must be another way to make a living doing what she loves. But Melanie lacks experience and has been hesitant to take a step in a different direction for years. The critical inner voice tells her, "You have no clue; others know better. You are not capable of forging your own path."*

The desire for autonomy and competence in human beings emerges from an early age. Even in the first attempts to grasp objects, move around, or communicate, we can see the yearning for freedom and self-determination through our own actions.

At its core, all learning, knowledge accumulation, the desire for growth and training, the urge to compare and compete with others, and the striving for advancement are manifestations of our longing for competence. We yearn to stand confidently in life, making decisions about our own path. Competence is crucial for breaking free from obligations and dependencies, providing us with a sense of security and self-assurance.

On the other hand, we also long to let go and surrender, wishing for someone to care for us just as we experienced in our childhood. During overwhelming moments in daily life, when challenges surpass our current capacity, or when we face grief, pain, or other difficulties, we desire the reassurance and assistance that comes from external support, resembling the nurturing care we receive from a maternal figure.

This longing for external guidance often stems from our hidden desire to be nurtured and cared for. We feel loved when someone takes care of us. However, as adults, we understand that we must primarily learn to care for ourselves, develop relationships based on equality, and take responsibility for our lives. We must walk hand in hand with others while maintaining our own boundaries and not relinquishing power and control over our personal sphere to others.

If our desire for autonomy has been violated in the past, leading to excessive mothering or abandonment, it can hinder our healthy development toward personal responsibility. It may leave us with unresolved wounds and triggers, causing us to unconsciously project our unmet longing for guidance onto our closest caregivers, such as our partners.

Take a moment to reflect on your current relationships, friendships, and connections with your parents. How do these relationships relate to the concept of competence? Do you feel a sense of equality and autonomy in your interactions? Do you notice any patterns indicating an inner conflict between autonomy and dependence? In which areas do you yearn to stand more firmly on your own feet? Do you believe in your ability to achieve this, or do you feel dependent on others for their affection and support? Are there any dependencies that keep you trapped in situations that no longer serve you well? What competencies do you need to liberate yourself from these constraints?

Consider also your engagement with the economic, social, and societal systems, whether it's in your profession or other everyday structures. Observe where you find yourself following external guidelines that you might prefer to leave behind once you have acquired the necessary competencies. What external guidelines provide you with a sense of security? How do you feel about the possibility of choosing a profession? Are you satisfied, or do you yearn for different activities? How do you perceive the hierarchy in your workplace or within student organizations? What skills do you wish to develop? Which political structures offer you guidance and security, and which laws would you like to see changed? Do you encounter any financial dependencies or obligations that make you feel less capable? What kind of support truly empowers you, and in what areas do you strive for autonomy?

Inspiration

Create a mind map showcasing the competencies that you actively utilize to shape your life. Include your positive character traits as well. Reflect on the goals you aim to achieve with these competencies.

In a separate mind map, illustrate the external requirements or societal expectations that diminish a significant portion of your personal responsibility and confine you within a social structure. This exercise will help you identify the dependencies you wish to break free from, while also recognizing the ones that align with the natural need for belonging and division of labor.

I Keep My Opinions to Myself - I Long for Connection

Examples:

- *Irene vividly remembers a childhood situation. At that time, the students exchanged small, trendy picture cards to expand their collections. Irene, being new to the class, was unfamiliar with the picture cards. Desperately, she sought guidance from her parents and neighbor children from other classes, but no one could provide the information she needed. Irene feared being exposed as an outsider. Eventually, someone shared more about the picture cards and even gave her a few. The next day, Irene was excited to participate in the card trading and showcase her knowledge. However, when she presented her cards, some children laughed and mocked her, pointing out that her cards were cheap copies and inferior. They dismissed her and belittled her understanding. Distraught, Irene ran away in tears.*

  This painful experience taught Irene that expressing her thoughts and wanting to belong would only result in ridicule and scorn.

  Deep down, Irene yearned to be part of the bigger picture and be valued for her expertise. However, the emotional pain from that incident still lingers, causing her to withhold her knowledge and opinions. She relies on self-selected sources for information but fears being shamed if she speaks up. Even in contentious discussions, she struggles to defend her perspective.

- *Sandra has long noticed a prevalent gossip culture within her circle of friends. She doesn't agree with it, but the fear of being excluded compels her to go along with it. Internally, she feels terrible, sacrificing her own boundaries to maintain acceptance within the group.*

- *Dawn has been married for twenty years, but she and her husband have grown apart. They have different goals and desires in many areas. However, Dawn is afraid to express her opinions and wishes because she fears confrontation. Despite sleeping in separate rooms as a way of creating distance, Dawn still loves her husband deeply and hopes for a reconciliation. She dreads the possibility of a loudly spoken separation and the associated feeling of radical rejection.*

Many people sacrifice their own boundaries, desires, and aspirations in order to fit in and be accepted. They long to be a part of the social fabric, but they hold back their true selves out of fear of rejection. In doing so, they deny themselves the opportunity to be truly known and to experience genuine connectedness. When we don't reveal our true thoughts and feelings, we miss out on the deep relationships we yearn for.

Often, we try to please people with whom we have little in common, attempting to win their approval. We may be unfamiliar with the feeling of being among like-minded individuals who can accept us as we are. Instead, we have become accustomed to proving ourselves and compromising our integrity to fit in.

Perhaps you can relate to this experience: feeling different from those around you and sensing a lack of genuine connection. You might find yourself having thoughts such as:

- ◆ "The others have no idea."
- ◆ "I am special. They just haven't realized it yet."
- ◆ "One day, I'll find my place."
- ◆ "There are people out there who will naturally understand me."

These thoughts indicate that you may have retreated into yourself, seeking safety and belonging in a place where you feel understood. You may feel that you were born into the wrong country, family, or culture and yearn for an environment that aligns better with who you are. If you have started to view your current environment negatively and have developed a judgmental stance, it can be helpful to engage in relaxed self-reflection by considering the following questions and prompts:

Inspiration

- ◆ Which culture would I most like to live in?
- ◆ If it were up to me, I would have parents who...
- ◆ If I could, I would prefer to have the following citizenship:...
- ◆ I hide these hidden character traits in my current environment:...
- ◆ If I were to simply show myself, I'm afraid that...
- ◆ I need... to unfold in a genuine and authentic way.
- ◆ For these reasons, in my opinion, it is not possible here:...
- ◆ I always look for others to blame since...

- Even then...
- At the core, I judge the people around me because...
- I long to...
- Could I allow myself to check if my fears really come true? What would be the best thing that could happen if I show myself as I am?
- If I could put aside my prejudices toward others, I would feel...
- What can I do to improve the tense atmosphere between me and my environment? Have I already done everything? What does it mean to give my best?

But perhaps the feeling of strangeness also manifests itself the other way around:

- I have to deny myself in order to belong.
- The others understood everything. I'm so bad and can't keep up.
- I have to work hard to hide what I really think and cover up what I cannot.
- I am overwhelmed and feel pressured to do something I don't want to do.

To explore your inner life, you can use the following prompts:

Inspiration

- In the past, no one ever thought I could...
- I always wished that..., but it never happened.
- I deeply long for...
- I admire with all my heart...
- I wish I could do as well... as...
- If I'm completely honest, I think... not so great.
- If there were people around me who were like I secretly am, we would represent the following interests together:...
- What does the thought trigger in me that I could perhaps inspire other people whom I know nothing about? With what secret interests and abilities could I enrich this world?
- What do I really think about what I am doing right now?
- What would my life be like if I refrained from any attempts to impress other people from now on?
- What do I most want to finally say no to?

Both forms of dissonance with your social environment are signs that you are experiencing difficulty in setting healthy, balanced boundaries and feeling comfortable with them. The feeling of disconnect with your environment indicates that, at some point in your life, likely unconsciously, you have resorted to extreme dissociation or strong adaptation as coping mechanisms to compensate for this pain. While these be-haviors may have served you well in childhood, in adulthood, they only lead to loneliness and a perpetual fear of rejection and exclusion. If you constantly find yourself longing to be somewhere else but fail to take action to prioritize self-care and seek an environment where you feel more at ease, you may inadvertently perpetuate the ongoing pain of not be-longing. You withdraw and isolate yourself despite craving connection.

On the other hand, if you tend to conform and suppress your authenticity, you may still feel lonely even when sur-rounded by a community. Deep down, you wonder if these people would truly accept and love you if you had the cour-age to fully reveal who you are.

While there are instances where it is necessary to prove our suitability for a relationship, job, responsibility, or shared task, it is important to recognize that such evaluations are fo-cused on our abilities in a specific context, not our inherent worth as individuals. Many individuals learned as children that criticism of their actions equated to criticism of their very being, leading them to believe that their true selves were not desired.

How, then, can we navigate this dilemma? How can we maintain our integrity, cultivate our own opinions, develop a strong sense of self, and simultaneously engage in the social fabric without compromising our authenticity? How do we embrace our fallibility and that of others without allowing fear to undermine our connections? When should we choose to leave, and when should we stay and show up?

The upcoming chapter will delve into these questions, shedding light on the path toward finding a harmonious balance between our individuality and our connection to the world around us.

Chapter 5

Embracing Your Authentic Self Through Boundaries

....

"Only those who know their limits know when to exceed them."

Rupert Schützbach

We yearn for both fusion and separation. Above all, we yearn to be authentically ourselves and simultaneously forge deep connections and loving relationships with others.

Your boundaries serve as the pathway to the sense of belonging you desire. This journey requires self-awareness, an understanding of your desires, and a willingness to explore the possibilities that exist within you and the world around you. It demands immense courage. By following this path, you assertively navigate through life, closing the door to everything that no longer serves your growth and well-being. However, this process is not without its share of pain. Even as you rejoice in freeing yourself from toxic behaviors and energy-draining influences, parting ways can be challenging. You may have become accustomed to unhealthy structures in your life for years, as they were once a familiar part of your survival strategy. They validated your beliefs and made you feel as though you were on a path that aligned with your self-perception. In congruence with what you believed about yourself, your experiences matched those beliefs.

Now, you have made the choice to embark on a new path. A path that honors the delicate beauty of the precious plants within your garden, carefully integrating them into the larger tapestry of your life. You are choosing to establish protective boundaries while remaining open to what resonates with your true self. Moreover, you have made the decision to lovingly and gently dismantle your inner defenses, allowing yourself the opportunity to embrace vulnerability and openness in areas where you seek growth and connection.

Saying No Confidently

Learning to say no with confidence is a skill that needs to be developed. It requires recognizing your own worth and being able to assert your own opinions and needs. The first step is understanding what you want to say no to. In this chapter, we will explore various areas where discussing and setting personal boundaries is important.

Toxic People
What do we mean by the term "toxic people"? Generally, we describe them as individuals who drain our energy to fulfill their own needs. They may consume our time, delegate tasks they don't want to do, offload their frustrations onto us and

exploit our strength, joy, and resources in various ways to gain an advantage for themselves.

However, the crucial point is that we often attribute the label of "toxic" solely to the person, becoming defensive and trying to protect ourselves. In doing so, we see them as the problem and may assign negative character traits to them, causing us to distance ourselves internally. But we must remember: It is not the responsibility of that person to maintain our boundaries; it is our responsibility to establish them from the beginning. It is our garden, our plants, and our space that they are encroaching upon, and we have allowed it. We have allowed our boundaries to be crossed by not clearly setting the bar.

At this point, it is important to ask ourselves: Why do we keep permitting these boundary violations? If it's not this person, it could be someone else. It's not solely about this particular individual being toxic; their behavior is toxic specifically to us. Another person could exhibit the same behavior, and we could be someone who either doesn't mind or can easily assert boundaries. Thus, it is the convergence of two individuals with behavior and weak boundaries that creates a toxic dynamic. Our challenge lies in not becoming further defensive or blaming ourselves but in working through and reinforcing our boundaries. Labeling someone as a "toxic person" won't help if we bid them farewell without clarifying our boundaries. Another person will come along and exploit the same vulnerabilities, causing similar disruptions. Why does this happen? It is because we have attracted them into our lives through our unchanging attitude. We often encounter what we radiate based on our inner beliefs about self-worth, self-efficacy, and our expectations of how others should treat us.

Your Valuable Time

Just like everyone else in this world, you have a limited amount of time allotted to you in life. While it's true that your lifestyle choices can impact the length of your life by a year or two, the true measure of time's value lies in how you spend it. A person who lives only ten years but fills that time with loving relationships, engaging pursuits, unforgettable experiences, and the fulfillment of dreams has utilized their time wisely. They have lived according to their personal needs and inclinations, free from the constraints of external systems or past wounds.

On the other hand, someone who rigidly adheres to self-imposed rules follows a predetermined path dictated by fear, fulfills obligations they are uncomfortable with, and lives up to the expectations of others may spend a hundred years on our beautiful planet and still feel deeply unhappy.

Your lifetime is the fundamental resource of your existence in this world. It is essential to recognize that time is finite and irretrievable. Does this realization sound disheartening? Quite the contrary! Embracing this profound understanding can empower you to take courageous steps, establish clear boundaries, and let go of anything in your life that prevents you from living healthily, happily, and fulfilled. This doesn't mean excluding everything that causes pain and discomfort or takes you out of your comfort zone. On the contrary, embracing life in its entirety means facing pain head-on, being open to it, surrendering, and allowing yourself to be vulnerable. It is through experiencing the full range of human emotions that we can fully embrace the present moment with open eyes and a loving heart.

Your pain can be transformative, a catalyst for healing and the birth of something new and beautiful. It is incomparable to the pain of an unlived life, wasted opportunities, disregarded boundaries, and abdicated responsibility. No one will ever thank you for sacrificing your precious life solely for the approval of your boss. Only when your work fulfills you and aligns with your heartfelt desires does it have a healing effect on your life. The moment you do things solely to earn love, recognition, and respect, you are no longer working for yourself but for others, seeking permission to exist. You perpetuate old wounds and allow your boss, parents, old friends, acquaintances, or societal norms to dictate your direction.

Your time is sacred, every single day, every minute, every decision within it. Grant yourself the permission to establish boundaries, for it is within these boundaries that you will truly make the most of your precious time.

Pre-Chewed
As humans, we have an innate desire to learn. Our brains crave novelty, expansion, and training. It naturally seeks to be engaged. While tradition and the tried-and-tested offer us security and roots in our lives, it is important to occasionally

question these traditions critically and evaluate their current relevance. Does what I have learned still hold true today? Has science progressed? Are there alternative sources of knowledge? Who are the individuals I have unquestioningly trusted? What truly interests me from within? In which areas do I seek new role models? Are there paths I want to explore without predefined guidelines? Where do my curiosity and longing take me?

Throughout different stages of life, there are moments when you consciously decide to let go of certain guidelines and embark on a personal journey of discovery. Such departures may involve some pain, depending on how those around you have positioned themselves and their openness to new, different, or contrasting ideas. However, you will always find new companions who share your path. It's not about reinventing the wheel or comparing yourself to others; rather, it's about listening to your heart and asking yourself: What does my heart tell me? What feels familiar and predetermined but no longer aligns with my personal truth? Where have I outgrown my previous experiences, and where do I want to further develop? And who are the individuals who support and share my enthusiasm?

At this point, you are likely to shift and redefine your boundaries. You may expand them outward, creating more space and exploring new horizons. This expansion can initially feel uncomfortable. You are claiming new territory within yourself that is yet unknown. However, it is yours, and you have the right to expand and unfold within it. During these phases, take the time to rediscover your ability to say "no" and confidently assert it. How can you do this? Through gaining personal experiences. While others may have shown you what to chew on, it is now time to open your own eyes and ears and explore your new terrain. It is through this exploration that you will discover when to say "no." You will see where it leads you and when it is time to gratefully pivot in a new direction.

Self-Worth

There comes a point in life when you face a decision - and the word "have to" is deliberately chosen here because this decision forms the basis for all your future conscious and unconscious boundary experiences. Decide to recognize and perceive your value as a human being, your worthiness of love, as fundamentally true and real. Initially, you may not be able to force yourself to feel that way, as experiences need to follow and support your new belief for your brain to actively form new neural pathways in favor of your perceived self-worth. However, you can make a conscious decision to believe that you are valuable, regardless of your current feelings. You can choose to reclaim the power within yourself to define what you believe about your worth, separate from the influence of your parents, past experiences, and caregivers. At times, you may need support and encouragement, and that's when you can seek out resources such as books, lectures, courses, and people who offer a new narrative about yourself. They use different language, behaviors, and thoughts about a person's worth, boundaries, and the potential of their future. If hurtful statements from your past, such as your father saying, "You'll never amount to anything," still resonate within you, it is your responsibility as an adult to examine the truth behind those words. You have the power to decide whether they hold any validity. Remember that they are just words from the mouth of someone who may have spoken out of their own hurt. You have the power to determine whether you give power to these words by continuing to believe in them because...

...your father said it.

...you have never experienced anything different.

...many others have said the same.

...it feels true.

You have the ability to rewrite your story by consciously embracing new, positive statements about yourself and allowing them to be true. Ask yourself empowering questions that challenge your old beliefs and open up new possibilities:

- Who says I truly cannot...?
- Is there any evidence supporting this belief?
- What if it were genuinely true that I am infinitely valuable?
- How would it feel if the affirmations in this book, that course... about my self-worth were actually true?
- What if my father, my mother, my friends... were mistaken in their negative statements because they are human and being wrong is part of being human?

It's important to align yourself with what feels true from your higher self, align it with your values and aspirations, and set a path that helps your emotional well-being anchor a new way of thinking and feeling. Remember that arriving at a new sense of self takes time. These words serve as a motivational reminder, not as a simplistic solution. Healing deep hurts and shifting our feelings about self-worth can take years as we navigate between our past experiences and our desired self-image.

Embrace the journey of self-acceptance, encompassing both your light and shadows, and make peace with who you are and who you aspire to become. Let your envisioned future and your present moment align. Even amidst self-doubt, you can continue on your path. It's about cultivating a fundamental attitude that says, "Although I often feel uncertain, deep down, I know that my past experiences no longer have to define me. There is something more for me. I may not feel it yet, and that's okay. I will keep reaching for it. I am valuable. I am loved. I am entitled to set boundaries. I have the right to say no. And if today didn't go as well as I hoped, I will try again tomorrow."

Everyday Affairs

Your daily choices shape the direction of your life and influence your experiences. When living in close proximity to others, your personal plans may clash with their needs and perspectives. Individuals who struggle with setting boundaries often put their own plans on hold and allow them to be disregarded all too frequently. This can lead to disruptions in family dynamics, friendships, or relationships. You find yourself constantly doing what others want while your own plans get postponed in the short term and eventually in the long term.

Confidently saying no begins with fully saying yes to your own plans and desires, valuing them as equal to any other plans. It is only on this level playing field that open discussions about prioritization, timing, and implementation can take place. However, past wounds may prevent you from fully expressing yourself and asserting your influence over what happens with your ideas. They may have led you to believe that you must wait your turn. Many people internalized this message during their childhood: "Wait for your turn to be heard." - "I don't have time right now. Maybe later." - "When I speak, you need to be quiet." - "As long as you're under my roof, you have no say here." Take a moment to reflect on the phrases that accompanied you during your upbringing and consider the feelings they still evoke in your everyday life today.

To practice confidently saying no, start by saying yes to everything that is important to you. Both joint future planning and your individual ideas and perceptions should be shaped not only by your partner or family members but by you as well. As you engage in this process, pay attention to any lingering feelings of guilt that may arise when asserting your plans as if they were selfish. Observe how many people naturally pursue their dreams and construct their daily lives without carrying this burden of guilt. This realization can help you understand that feeling guilty is not normal or necessary. Imagine how liberating it would feel to bring your plans to the table with a sense of freedom, playfulness, and relaxation. Practice clear and effective communication:

"I would like to do this or that today. Who would like to join me?"

"This particular time doesn't work for me. How about...?"

"No, I'm not comfortable with that today. I would prefer..."

"You're welcome to go on your own. I will join you in due time..."

Inspiration

Practice a confident " no" with your body:

Find a comfortable spot in the middle of a room and take a few deep breaths to center yourself.

Now, one by one, imagine various situations where you would like to confidently say no. Here are some examples:

- Constant expectations from your parents
- Disrespectful behavior from your children
- Persuasion attempts from your partner
- Overtime demands at work
- Salesman's attempts to persuade you in a shoe store
- ...

Stand tall, straighten your posture, and lift your chin. Let your eyes convey determination as you feel the power of your no rising from your feet, traveling up through your legs, belly, chest, arms, neck, and into your head. Embrace your no and embody it fully. Stomp your foot, vigorously shake your head, make a dismissive arm movement that feels authentic, and loudly and confidently say:

"No! No! No!"

Avoid adding explanations, filler words, or niceties. Just assertively say no. Repeat this exercise for any situations that come to mind and feel relevant to you.

Afterward, turn around and leave the room without looking back.

Take a short break, and a few hours later, reflect on your experience during the exercise. Note what emotions it triggered in you and how you felt in the hours that followed.

Feel free to repeat this exercise as often as you like to further strengthen your ability to assertively say no.

Competently Charting Your Own Path

Competence involves having a clear understanding of what you are doing. Fortunately, our lives are always full of surprises. Nothing remains stagnant, everything undergoes change, and we can never anticipate all the risks or have complete control over the future.

However, we can follow an inner guiding thread and set goals that align with our true nature. We can make decisions with integrity that keep us on our path and true to ourselves. Even when the exact destination of this path is unclear, we can consciously make choices and take responsibility for the outcomes. Competence in navigating our own path means not relinquishing it to others who may think they know better.

Developing competence requires trust. Trust in our own capacity to be wise, discerning, and attentive—to listen to the inner voice that guides us with the right signals. Those who trust themselves demonstrate competence in taking charge of their own lives. Our individual path becomes our greatest responsibility as we mature. Individuals striving for mental, spiritual, and physical well-being find comfort in this competence and celebrate their own successes in fully embracing life. They no longer blame others for their circumstances. This competence empowers us to set clear boundaries and communicate, "This is my space. I determine how I want to live, what I believe in, and where I invest my energy." Those who are truly aware of their competencies often do not even need to articulate this with words. They radiate a sense of security and trust, and those around them can sense it—this person is at peace with themselves and trust their own ability to lead their own life.

Competence in One's Own Healing Journey

Healing involves the process of becoming whole, restoring balance, and establishing connections. Physically, mentally, and spiritually, we seek healing when our condition no longer aligns with the natural state from which we, as humans, originally emerged.

The subject of healing is vast, with countless perspectives and personal truths circulating in the world. The market is filled with a multitude of books, sciences, belief systems, traditions, and convictions. Some of these viewpoints clearly contradict each other, while others can be integrated. Certain approaches are presented as the sole path, while others are dismissed as charlatanism. Each perspective brings forth its own set of supposed proofs or underlying truths to support its stance.

As adults, we can only find our own way by allowing ourselves to discover our personal truth in relation to our own lives and healing journey. It is not beneficial to adopt something simply because we perceive the source as wiser, more experienced, or as a figure of power to whom we feel inferior. If something within us quietly reminds us that the suggested solution does not resonate with our inner truth, it is wise to listen. It is important to seek information, consult experts, and place trust in institutions and knowledge that surpass our own in matters of physical, mental, and spiritual health. However, our intuition and gut feelings play a crucial role in determining the extent to which we trust others. Both rationality and intuition should complement each other. In this day and age, we are fortunate to have access to a variety of sciences, belief systems, and traditions that can contribute to our desired restoration and healing.

Your self-confidence can greatly flourish when you make decisions for your inner and outer well-being and take responsibility for the direction of your own path. What may benefit one person could be harmful to another, and vice versa. Take control of your health. Engage in research, question, and continue exploring until you feel empowered and capable of deciding if and who should assist you, where to seek guidance, and even how to define "health" in a way that resonates with you personally.

Not only is healing and health crucial to your self-awareness, but this mindset extends to all areas of your life. Practice making conscious, informed decisions. Embrace the process of maturing. Joyfully embrace your responsibilities. Allocate your resources, give direction, pivot when necessary, and trust your own judgment. By doing so, you will experience yourself as effective, empowered, and in control of your own life. This will create a strong character profile, and others will perceive and respect your boundaries more clearly and distinctly.

Competently Plan Your Future

During your childhood, your parents, based on their beliefs, took on the responsibility of preparing you for a successful life. Their intention was typically to equip you with the necessary skills for your future. However, as you grew older, you began to explore how your own desires and personal growth aligned with the plans your parents and guardians had envisioned for you. You started to differentiate yourself and made efforts to forge your own path. Throughout childhood and adolescence, there were phases in which you sought autonomy, sometimes more, sometimes less, and rebelled against the ideas and guidelines of your environment.

As an adult, the focus shifts away from simply setting yourself apart to discover or better understand yourself. Mature life planning involves less comparison with others and more alignment with your own inner compass, independent of how those around you live their lives. You develop the competence to be your own yardstick and assess your goals based on your own desires, talents, and values. Competence entails looking within yourself and not seeking validation from external sources.

Once you confidently and maturely plan your future from within, you can then engage with your environment and seek opportunities where your vision harmonizes with a larger whole. It is only natural and healthy to collaborate with others rather than pursue your individual path in isolation. However, true collaboration can only happen when you have taken charge of your own future. Remember to assert your self-assured "no" and practice the competence of maintaining your own stance. View any conflicts with people or the need to change your internal direction as an opportunity to take ownership of your future. Embrace your goals as if they have already been accomplished. The more you can embody your desires, the more you will recognize your ability to shape your own life, regardless of the circumstances around you.

Competently Choose and Navigate Relationships

During your childhood, relationships may have felt like something that happened to you. Unwanted relationships were imposed upon you, such as:

- Visiting an unpleasant aunt
- Mandatory vacation time with grandparents
- Depressing meal times with family
- Sibling and parental conflicts
- ...

Desired relationships also developed through fortunate circumstances, such as:

- Meeting a new neighbor after moving
- Making friends at school
- Connecting with the children of your parent's friends whom you happened to like
- ...

In many cases, as a child, you had little control over these experiences. You couldn't decide if your family moved, who your parents befriended, if others liked you, or if you were placed in the same class as your best friend.

However, as an adult, you have the power to say yes or no to certain circumstances. While you may not be able to immediately change a situation that is bothering you, you have the ability to reflect on it and make far-reaching decisions independently, free from dependence on your parents or other individuals who used to determine where and with whom you spent your time.

Many people have internalized this old pattern of dependence on others to such an extent that the path to healthy autonomy becomes challenging. However, developing competence in relationships can lead to an unimaginable degree of freedom and fulfillment. It is a journey well worth taking.

Inspiration

Create a wish list of areas in which you would like to develop competence through education and knowledge.

In a separate list, identify the areas in which you already feel competent and confident, regardless of others' opinions.

Choose a favorite area from your lists and stand in front of a mirror. Speak to yourself in short sentences, explaining why you are competent and why you can wholeheartedly trust yourself.

Rooted Living: Embracing Individuality

How can we embrace our individuality while feeling connected and rooted? What do we want to be rooted in and connected to? How can we maintain a sense of connection while asserting our boundaries?

Establishing healthy boundaries becomes possible when we have a sense of belonging. Feeling secure and knowing that our boundaries will be respected, without the fear of losing relationships, home, or a sense of belonging, allows us to truly feel grounded.

To achieve this, it is crucial that we develop the competence to shape our lives with personal responsibility. When this foundation is in place, we naturally find the people and places where we can root ourselves. This may involve sharing a certain worldview, fostering deep friendships, or relying on other pillars that provide us with a sense of security. With such grounding, there is no need to shut ourselves off from our surroundings or pass judgment. Defensive attitudes and excessive focus on our limitations arise only when we do not feel safe, comfortable, and secure within ourselves and our immediate environment. Those who have strong roots can confidently soar without perceiving the sky as a threat.

Each person approaches rootedness differently. We seek various anchors that feel like home, allowing us to develop autonomous attitudes and chart our own unique paths, fostering a sense of individuality. Rootedness is not about right or wrong; it is about feeling safe, secure, and aligned with our values.

By being aware of our values, we can choose environments that support and share those values. This enables us to find communities and spheres where we feel anchored. Since everyone expresses themselves differently based on their personal history, worldview, and values, there are countless directions to explore: religious affiliations, political beliefs, a sense of belonging to certain places, specific lifestyles, or social structures. Your anchor is a unique composition of what holds significance for you.

Some individuals prioritize the people they live with over the physical location. Others cannot fathom leaving their birthplace, cherishing lifelong friendships, or adhering to spiritual practices, recurring rituals, or inherited traditions. There are also those who root themselves in their talents, passions, or vocations.

Inspiration

Begin by creating a mind map that identifies five areas of your life that provide you with a sense of roots and security. Write them down and then summarize the emotions and emotional states that you associate with each of these areas.

Once you have identified these five areas, it's important to assess whether they continue to fulfill your current needs and support your development. Ask yourself if you still feel comfortable in these areas or if you have a desire for change but are afraid of uprooting yourself by leaving them.

Next, consider which other areas could potentially become new sources of roots for you. Explore possibilities that align with your convictions and ideals of life, providing you with a sense of identity and support.

Additionally, take into account your natural rhythm, which includes both a desire for freedom, change, and autonomy, as well as a need for security and rootedness. These inner states often alternate and intertwine in a dance-like pattern, unique to each individual. Some people may embark on months-long travel adventures, only to settle firmly in one place for a few months afterward. Others may maintain the same home for decades while finding freedom through exciting projects, relationships, or hobbies.

By understanding and honoring your natural rhythm, you can discover how to follow your inner longing in a balanced and healthy way, meeting your needs effectively. This exploration will also help you identify areas where outbursts or stagnation occur, which do not serve you or bring true fulfillment.

It is important to have an understanding of your own needs for autonomy and rootedness. This self-awareness forms the foundation for a self-determined life with clear boundaries.

Examples:

- *Simon has a clear understanding of her desire for freedom, particularly in the realm of travel. She doesn't feel the need for a permanent home but seeks stability in committed, long-term relationships or solitude. When faced with opportunities that do not align with her vision of a stable partnership, she sets boundaries and confidently says no, even if she genuinely likes the person involved.*

- *Finn finds security and stability in established habits and a structured daily routine. He values the freedom to work independently and on his own terms. As a result, he turns down a well-paid job offer that would require him to adhere to fixed working hours. For Finn, the cost of sacrificing his freedom outweighs the financial gain.*

- *Andrea places great importance on relationships that foster deep, meaningful conversations. She sets boundaries with individuals who only seek casual chit-chat and passing time. Andrea prioritizes investing her time in people genuinely interested in exploring topics at a profound level.*

- *Desiree has decided to stop attending family parties and Christmas celebrations. The pressure to buy presents and the overall tense and depressing atmosphere within her large family circle have taken a toll on her well-being. By establishing this boundary, she breaks away from years of family tradition that no longer aligns with her needs. Desiree seeks rootedness by nurturing strong friendships and explores the idea of spending quality time together during Christmas without burdensome expectations and materialistic focus.*

- *Annette has been employed by the same company for two decades. Despite personal challenges and low self-esteem, the stability of a regular income provided her with a sense of security and rootedness. However, she faces bullying at work and eventually decides to set a boundary by saying no and resigning from her position. This choice creates a newfound space for Annette to reestablish her roots. She embarks on a journey of self-discovery, realizing that she needs to cultivate a stronger sense of self-anchor.*

Chapter 6
Practical Self-Love

"Personal boundaries can be explored and, at times, crossed recklessly, but it is up to me to decide when they've gone too far."

Detlev Wentzel

As the guardian of your territory, you have the power to decide who may enter your garden, when they may visit, or even stay permanently. You establish the rules and teach others about the customs of your world.

In order to convey this authentically and effectively, it is crucial that you first find inner peace and learn to provide yourself with the love and care you desire from others. By setting the standard for how you wish to be treated, you radiate your self-worth. It is unrealistic to expect others to give you what you have not yet cultivated within yourself. Your actions and demeanor reflect what you value. If you are not truly convinced of certain aspects of your own way of living and behaving, it will permeate the atmosphere around you, and your boundaries will be more easily disregarded.

Example:

Stefanie finds herself questioning why her children consistently display careless, disobedient, and mischievous behavior towards her. She has dedicated years of effort to being a loving, calm, and balanced mother.

However, her children increasingly push the boundaries, openly disregarding her instructions and even resorting to yelling and name-calling. Stefanie is at a loss and unsure of what to do next. It is during a coaching session that she has a profound realization:

Stefanie harbors a deep sense of anger and disappointment stemming from the fact that she has consistently placed her own life and interests on the back burner in order to prioritize her children's well-being. While she aspires to cultivate joy, peace, and balance, her children unconsciously sense a different energy that contradicts her intentions. They pick up on the unexpressed anger, powerlessness, and discontent that Stefanie directs towards herself. Consequently, her children mirror these emotions back to her through their challenging behavior. At first glance, it may seem like a transgression of boundaries, but Stefanie is being treated in this way because she fails to acknowledge her own feelings and thus neglects her own boundaries in the presence of others. She serves as a role model for her children, who are not solely influenced by her words but also by the unspoken emotions that emanate from Stefanie's presence.

Self-Care

Self-care forms the foundation for effectively caring for others. When your own cup is filled and overflowing, you can extend care to others without depleting yourself. Establishing healthy boundaries ensures that your care remains sustainable, preventing feelings of exhaustion. By prioritizing self-care, you attain a sense of fulfillment, strength, and energy to make a positive impact in areas that resonate with you.

Defining self-care based on your individual needs and preferences sets a personal standard for your life. You establish the benchmark that aligns with your well-being. Taking good

care of yourself may manifest as frequent vacations or starting each day in a peaceful manner. It can mean desiring a
world where no one treats you rudely or expecting people to
demonstrate excessive kindness and love.

Observing others practice self-care can be inspiring. However, it is essential to recognize that projecting someone else's
standards onto yourself and blindly imitating their approach
is unproductive. Each person's circumstances, temperament,
wants, and needs are unique, as are their limitations and pri-
orities. Embrace self-care practices that resonate with your
individuality and honor your personal journey.

Inspiration

Create a series of number rays depicting a spectrum
from negative to zero and transitioning to positive. Utilize these different representations to conduct a realis-
tic self-assessment of how well you are taking care of
yourself in the various areas of focus. This evaluation
should be based on your individual perception, without
comparing it to external standards.

Example:

Fitness

<-------------------------------------I------------------------->
- Neutral +

Nutrition

<-------------------------------------I------------------------->
- Neutral +

Close Friendships

<----------------------------------I------------------------->

- Neutral +

Conflicts Resolution

<----------------------------------I------------------------->

- Neutral +

Mental Development

<----------------------------------I--------------------------->

- Neutral +

Working Conditions

<----------------------------------I--------------------------->

- Neutral +

Everyday Planning

<----------------------------------I--------------------------->

- Neutral +

Emotional Needs

<----------------------------------I--------------------------->

- Neutral +

Housing Situation

<----------------------------------I--------------------------->

- Neutral +

Communication
<------------------------------------I------------------------->
- Neutral +

Finance
<------------------------------------I------------------------->
- Neutral +

Identify which areas hold particular importance to you. When do you feel that you are effectively practicing self-care, and what does that entail for you? Is it sufficient to merely get by, or do you aspire to experience abundance in certain aspects of your life? Do you yearn to release any guilt associated with setting higher standards for yourself?

Many individuals have been conditioned to believe that desiring more than just the bare minimum is presumptuous. This often manifests in relation to finances, where they secretly wish to be wealthy and have an abundance of money, yet deny themselves the permission to embrace this desire. They feel selfish or judge themselves negatively for entertaining such thoughts. Consequently, they maintain a standard of living that remains in the negative range or at best neutral, instead of moving towards abundance.

> **Remember:** When you prioritize only your basic needs and attempt to remain inconspicuous by setting low standards for fulfilling your needs, you often find yourself feeling taken advantage of and overlooked by others. Your boundaries are frequently violated because you have little to offer beyond what you require for yourself—and yet, you still give. It is only by living in abundance that you can genuinely give to others.
>
> *Only when you live in abundance can you truly give to others.*

Communication

Communication is the key to taking personal responsibility for establishing and maintaining boundaries in interpersonal relationships. Those who can effectively communicate their boundaries and assertively defend them make a significant contribution to creating successful relationships based on equality.

Clear and precise communication is crucial for conveying our boundaries. It is important to recognize that approximately eighty percent of communication is nonverbal. Only a small portion of our message is conveyed through words. The majority is expressed through our presence, facial expressions, gestures, body language, and emotional state. These aspects are difficult to conceal, and they speak louder than words.

Therefore, it is essential to attain clarity within ourselves regarding what we want to communicate, convey, and achieve.

When we have clarity internally, others can also sense it, and they will take our words seriously.

Before expressing your thoughts clearly, take the time to reflect on your inner self. It can be helpful to focus on one or two areas in your life where you frequently experience boundary violations. Ask yourself the following questions:

- What exactly is happening? What are people doing that crosses my boundaries?
- What emotions does this trigger within me?
- What would I most like to express or communicate?
- Where do my boundaries lie on the number line at this moment?
- Do I want to maintain my boundaries at their current level, or do I aspire to set higher ones and move into the positive range?
- What might be the reasons behind not allowing myself to have this desire until now? Are there any limiting beliefs that have influenced me?
- What should be the new standard for my life? How can I support myself in making a clear decision and letting go of the old standard?

Examples:

- *Robin desires a job that allows him to showcase his capabilities and leadership qualities. He envisions taking on more responsibility and making a significant impact. However, during job interviews, his insecurities and nervousness overshadow his true potential. Instead of expressing his secret qualities, he com-*

municates a sense of uncertainty and a hope for acceptance. This is evident both in his body language, such as sitting with crossed legs and half-folded arms while nervously shifting back and forth and in his choice of words, which often include terms like "possibly," "maybe," and "one could consider whether," and "I hope."

Despite recently completing further training and acquiring valuable knowledge and expertise, Robin tends to forget the content he had prepared when faced with questioning from management during interviews. He recalls the times when he didn't receive much respect and gradually loses confidence in himself. Although he may manage to express fragments of the aspirations he intended to convey to the employer, his inner mindset no longer supports his words. Consequently, the initially promising atmosphere fades away, and the potential employers start adopting a more provocative tone in their questions. Robin begins to feel interrogated and cornered, resulting in a loss of mutual understanding and an erosion of the perceived equality. Ultimately, this dynamic leads to a negative outcome of the conversation.

♦ *For some time now, Maria has been desiring to create more distance between herself and her mother. Her mother puts pressure on her with a victim mentality, expecting regular calls and visits and bombarding Maria with a range of topics: illnesses, annoyances, unsolicited advice, and constant critiques about Maria's life situation.*

Maria's attempts to communicate her boundaries to her mother in a friendly manner have been hindered by unclear and overly cautious communication. As a child, Maria learned that any attempt to assert her own boundaries would result in her mother feeling attacked and offended. Consequently, her mother was never able to truly hear, accept, and respect Maria's boundaries.

Even today, Maria finds herself trapped in a cycle of struggling to find clear and assertive words, fearing that it will lead to arguments and ultimately result in her apologizing to her mother. She desperately hopes that her mother will understand the underlying message between the lines, but every hesitation creates an opening that her mother fills with her own stories, depleting Maria of her time, strength, and energy. While Maria's desired limit lies in the positive range—preferring little to no contact with her mother for a period of time—she settles for internal withdrawal and shorter phone calls. However, this approach hardly diminishes the toxic influence of her mother's behavior, leading Maria to experience increasing levels of stress, nervousness, and anger. In reality, her boundary has slipped into the negative range.

People like Robin and Maria yearn for freedom, to authentically live as their true selves, and to break free from their internal limitations. However, their old patterns and self-imposed restrictions hinder them from permitting themselves to reveal their true selves and desires to the outside world.

By not clearly communicating their boundaries, Robin and Maria leave themselves vulnerable and increase the risk of not being heard or respected. Consequently, their boundaries continue to be violated. Hiding behind unclear communication does not provide them any advantage. Many individuals only decide to disclose their boundaries when the weight of their suffering becomes unbearable. It is at this point that they gather the courage to shed their old ways and liberate themselves from their internal limitations and unhealthy relationships.

Clear communication is a skill that can be developed through practice. It involves maintaining empathy to preserve connection while simultaneously expressing one's own perspective in a clear and unequivocal manner. By doing so, the other person is not burdened with the responsibility of deciphering one's boundaries between the lines. This approach helps avoid conflicts and misunderstandings. Simplifying, providing concrete information, and sticking to factual statements are helpful strategies for effective communication.

Here are some examples that clearly convey one's intentions:

"I have decided to... (share point of view)."

"In the next two months (specify time), I would like to..."

"I'm still considering... (keeping the other person informed). I will inform you by... (specify time)."

"When we argue, I feel... (emotional revelation). I would appreciate it if we could... (constructive suggestion)."

"I do not want you to take my belongings without asking."

"I would like to help you by... (providing a specific proposal instead of a vague offer)."

Miscommunication often arises when one seeks an agreement but internally resists or rebels against the consensus because it surpasses their personal boundaries. In such instances, one may verbally say yes, while not fully supporting it, and the other person senses that something is amiss.

Example:

Miles has found himself in repeated open conflicts with his mother. She insists that he "grow up and get a job" at the age of 28. However, Miles desires to establish boundaries and no longer be controlled by his mother's expectations. He attempts to have a conversation with her, seeking a peaceful resolution and asking her to understand that he is responsible for his own life. Unfortunately, his mother is solely concerned with her reputation and fears becoming the subject of gossip among the neighbors if her son doesn't secure a job. While Miles also wishes for progress in his professional career, he feels a tightness within him at the thought of his mother winning. Consequently, during their discussions, he struggles to assert himself assertively and draw a clear line, making it clear that his decisions are not made solely to please her.

The surface issue of the job search is merely a manifestation of a deeper conflict between mother and child. The ongoing dispute serves as the stage where the true conflict unfolds and is further fueled by ambivalent communication. Miles yearns to be recognized as an adult and for his mother to release him and trust in his abilities. Conversely, his mother harbors secret feelings of guilt from Miles' childhood and seeks val-

idation as a mother by witnessing his success, hoping it will alleviate her sense of failure. Indirectly, she places the burden of her emotional well-being on Miles and expects him to resolve her internal conflict.

In such cases, two options emerge that can lead to clear communication:

Both parties decide to share their inner feelings during the conflict and together delve deeper into the root cause of the issue. They employ clear, nonviolent communication techniques. Miles learns to articulate his defensiveness and communicates to his mother that it signifies his internal boundary. He no longer wishes to engage in discussions with his mother about how he lives his life. It doesn't mean that he isn't concerned about his future.

Miles' mother's primary responsibility is to respect and accept this boundary. She can express this verbally and refrain from formulating any further reproaches or expectations in future conversations. If she wishes, she can also reflect on her feelings of guilt without necessarily communicating them to her son.

Alternatively, it can be beneficial to take a step back and individually address the inner conflicts. Both parties may temporarily separate to work on their own personal growth without the need for endless conversations.

In order to determine the right course of action in such cases, it is important to keep the ultimate goal in mind: Do you want to strengthen the relationship, preserve it, end it, or take it to a new level? What is the underlying purpose of the conflict? Do both parties need to agree on every aspect of each other's lives? How can understanding be fostered that maintains the connection while allowing each party to lead their own lives?

When it comes to close friendships or long-lasting partnerships that aim for growth, it becomes even more crucial to express feelings and emotions within a safe environment. Therefore, it is essential to establish a conversational culture where all involved parties strive to communicate clearly and assert their own boundaries.

To facilitate respectful communication, you can engage in an exercise with a trusted friend or a coach to gain insight into your own position and boundaries in conflict situations.

Inspiration

You need:

- A three-meter-long rope
- An exercise partner

Stand in the middle of a room and hold the rope in your hand. Lay it out in a circle around you. Notice the amount of space between you and the rope. This space represents your sanctuary, the garden where your personal boundaries exist, your home, your privacy.

Now ask your exercise partner to walk towards you from outside the circle at various speeds - sometimes fast, sometimes slow, sometimes from the front, sometimes from behind. Tune into your inner feelings and sensations, and when you feel that the person is getting too close, say "stop" to indicate they should halt.

This exercise enables you to connect with your internal sense of when you reach your personal limit, prompting the "stop" feeling. By engaging in this practice, you can become more aware of when your inner boundaries are being reached and the associated feeling of needing to halt. Consider the following scenarios: Is the other person moving too quickly, failing to include you in the process? Are you unable to see them, causing you to feel unsafe? Are they moving too slowly, testing your patience? Is it someone you don't want to be close to, or perhaps someone you allow to get too close?

If the person crosses your red line (represented by the rope) before you say "stop," take the opportunity to reflect on the following:

- Is the space between you and your red line, signifying your privacy, too small? Do you desire to move the rope outward and expand the space around you?
- Do you struggle to assert your boundaries and say "no"? What fears may arise within you? What apprehensions do you have about setting a limit?

> ◆ Do you actually want the person to come closer? Why do you allow them to cross your red line? How can you maintain contact and connection without compromising your sense of self?

It may not always be possible to perform this exercise directly with the person involved in the actual conflict. However, you can engage in the exercise mentally after trying it once with someone else. By doing so, you can gain insight into your feelings towards the person and identify the boundaries you would like them to respect. Recognizing the distance between you and the other person allows you to choose a communication approach that aligns with the dynamics of your current relationship situation.

Miles was constantly tempted to share details about his life and current situation with his mother. Despite her consistent criticism of his decisions, he felt an obligation to keep her informed. In doing so, he unknowingly reinforced the pattern between them, allowing his mother to comment on his affairs and interfere.

Through the rope exercise, Miles realized that he actually desired a greater physical distance from his mother. He envisioned her standing several meters away, perhaps on the opposite side of the street. In this imaginary scenario, they would exchange friendly greetings, such as "Good morning" and "Isn't the weather nice?" before continuing on their separate paths. In contrast, his perception of their real interactions involved his mother constantly following him, exerting control over his every action, and he willingly shared everything with her.

To change this dynamic, Miles made a shift in his communication approach. He stopped divulging his plans and decisions to his mother. Instead, he established a routine of calling her every two to three weeks for a brief conversation, not exceeding 15 minutes. During this time, he also chose not to answer her calls for several months. By doing so, Miles expanded his personal boundaries, creating more space for himself, while his mother figuratively switched sides of the street. Although the process took time, they eventually developed a friendly relationship.

In hindsight, it became apparent that the boundaries Miles set had a positive impact on his mother as well. She was relieved from the burden of expending her energy in constant worry and control over her son. This newfound freedom allowed her to refocus on her own well-being. She released the tension and began contemplating the questions she had previously directed towards Miles: What do I want to do? How do I envision spending the upcoming years?

Authenticity

Authenticity in behavior and appearance entails accepting everything that resides within you and allowing it to exist. This includes embracing both the light and dark aspects, acknowledging your weaknesses and vulnerabilities, recognizing blind spots, experiencing joy and enthusiasm, and embodying your soulfulness and touchability. It requires a deep and wholehearted YES to all parts of yourself. As you undergo processes of learning and gaining experiences, your sense of self will evolve and change. However, you can always find a resounding affirmation of your being that encompasses every transformation.

On the contrary, a lack of authenticity arises when one only reveals and lives a fraction of oneself to the outside world or attempts to completely embody someone else. Those who cannot wholeheartedly accept and love themselves tend to deny, negate, and repress certain aspects of themselves. This inner conflict leads to a growing inhibition to express and showcase their true selves. When someone is divided within themselves, it becomes challenging to be present and connected during interactions with others.

Rarely do we align our internal sense of self with what we exhibit to the external world. Nevertheless, the goal of personal development is to bridge this gap and cultivate an authentic way of living and expressing ourselves.

Many individuals who struggle with authenticity notice that their behavior significantly varies depending on who they are with. Different people elicit specific aspects of their being, which they then emphasize, often to please the other person. As a result, other dimensions of their true selves fade into the background.

Examples:

- *When Annika reunites with her old friends from the past, she conceals the fact that she has undergone personal growth and transformation. She reverts to speaking and behaving as she did back then, discussing topics like soccer and typical pub conversations. Despite these no longer aligning with her current life, Annika hesitates to approach the encounter as the present-day*

Annika—a woman with a family, residing in the city, and passionate about sustainability. If she could openly express her true self and still cherish the memories of old times, there would be no issue. However, Annika feels compelled to pretend in order to avoid being marginalized within her old social circle.

♦ *Michelle yearns for friendships in which she can freely discuss her personal and family life. She observes seemingly blissful families all around her while she grapples with challenges within her own partnership. Consequently, Michelle conforms to the image of happiness, fearing rejection and shame. She refrains from being authentic and keeps her private life hidden, even from close friends. Opening up becomes a daunting task for her. Eventually, she realizes that she is surrounded by social circles that don't align with her true self. She begins to seek connections with individuals who also value authenticity. Setting a boundary, Michelle cuts off contact with those who require her to maintain a facade in order to be accepted.*

To some extent, it is normal that we don't reveal every aspect of ourselves to everyone. That is why we maintain different friendships with different people, discussing various topics and sharing different commonalities. However, when certain parts of our personality are consistently hidden, suppressed, or pushed away to the point where discomfort arises, it often indicates a deep insecurity within ourselves. We may question whether we are deserving of love and acceptance for who we truly are. It is acceptable if your girlfriend isn't interested in discussing soccer, but if you feel compelled to deny your love for soccer in order to be accepted, it becomes difficult to maintain authenticity in that relationship.

There are individuals who consistently attract people into their lives based solely on how they respond to specific aspects that they emphasize, either intensely accepting or intensely rejecting while keeping everything else hidden.

Example:

Tania is in search of a new partner. After each initial meeting, she excitedly shares with her friend about the new acquaintance, praising his courteous behavior, charming ways, and the wonderful experiences they have shared. However, a recurring pattern emerges within a few weeks: Tania notices a change in her new boyfriend's demeanor. He becomes increasingly unfriendly, less attentive, and appears to be losing interest. In response, Tania seeks out conversations with him, trying to explain why she is deserving of his consistent interest and care. She asks him questions such as:

- *Could it be that you are afraid of getting closer?*
- *Could it be that you are preoccupied with work?*
- *Could it be that my inner strength is intimidating you?*

Rather than ending the relationship and establishing clear boundaries and expectations, Tania chooses to stay in the connection until the other person communicates that their initial interest is not as genuine as she had hoped. It is only then that the other person walks away, leaving Tania questioning what went wrong. Tania typically believes in her strength as a woman and feels deserving of being a priority in someone else's life. However, once she establishes a connection with someone, she tends to shift into a role of trying to help the other person like her, transforming into their coach and advisor. Deep inside, an old belief system takes hold, whispering, "If you don't make the other person see your worth, they won't recognize it on their own. You don't deserve to find a wonderful man who can appreciate your value." Moreover, Tania seems to lack genuine conviction in her own strength and inner light. At times, a troubling thought creeps in, "What if my partner realizes that I may appear great, but deep down, I'm just an ordinary person?"

Tania finds security in the moments when she feels confident and empowered, attracting positive attention from others, such as receiving smiles and phone number requests from men on the street. However, as the connection deepens and becomes more intimate, she feels compelled to reveal her vulnerabilities and weaknesses. This triggers her belief system, which asserts, "If you present yourself as small, you will drive people away, but if you are doing well, you can attract them." The man senses this hidden belief and reflects it back to her through his avoidance and diminishing respect.

Just like Tania, many people find themselves in an in-between space where they showcase their strengths to the outside world while keeping their weaknesses hidden. This often leads to sending mixed and unclear signals, creating confusion both for themselves and others in terms of establishing clear boundaries.

Tania wishes for a lifelong partnership but often gives off the impression that she only stands strong during good times when she feels confident and secure. However, as soon as insecurity arises, she compromises her own integrity and projects her doubts onto the other person. She questions whether they still recognize her or if they are afraid of getting closer. In reality, it is Tania herself who is afraid. As a result, her relationships consistently reach the same outcome. She is only content with her positive attributes and has yet to fully embrace her shadow side. This lack of clear boundaries becomes evident when she tolerates unfriendly and disrespectful behavior precisely when she needs kindness the most.

Now, it is crucial for Tania to deeply reflect on herself in these areas and learn to accept herself as a normal person. She must allow herself to be average and expect that another person can find happiness in that. As she cultivates this sense of self-worth, a transformation can occur. Her boundaries become clear, and she no longer attracts men seeking fleeting adventures and superficial connections. Her environment perceives her as a person with both light and shadow from the beginning, someone who embraces her entirety and expects to be loved in her wholeness. Consequently, she will attract men who embrace all aspects of her and are comfortable with their own shadows.

During this process, Tania realizes that she struggles to accept a man with imperfections and is apprehensive about his vulnerabilities. Because she has not allowed herself to be vulnerable, she may not have felt secure with a vulnerable man and may have unconsciously been waiting for a flawless knight in shining armor.

If Tania lets go of this idealized image and grants permission for everything that resides within her, she will also find a man who embodies the same level of clarity. This is the first step towards growth and learning together for both individuals.

Inspiration

Writing Exercise:

Pick a topic where you currently feel disconnected from your true self and struggle to act authentically. Complete the following sentence starters to help you tap into your genuine attitude, opinions, and separate yourself from external influences that may confuse you.

- If I'm being completely honest, I feel...
- What I actually want to say is...
- If there were no negative consequences, I would...
- I am not willing to pay the price...
- I would give anything to have...
- If I were to paint my inner life in colors, it would actually be... I feel that the color of the outer situation... doesn't resonate with me right now.
- I would most like to say to... that...
- ... keeps me from doing so.
- If I decide today to be authentic and honest...

Manipulation

"I always feel like I'm being externally controlled; my life doesn't feel like my own."

"My attitude and opinion change immediately as soon as I am around this person. They make such compelling points."

"I adapt to them so much, even though I don't want to. I feel like I can hardly compete with that."

"Sometimes I just want to get away from them to rediscover myself, but as soon as they enter the room, I'm overwhelmed with joy."

"I've changed since I've been with them. I hardly recognize myself anymore, and it doesn't feel good."

"I am always at a loss for words; conversations confuse me. I feel like I can't think straight anymore."

Manipulation involves the covert influence of other people on your thoughts, feelings, behaviors, and actions. Individuals can engage in manipulative behavior both consciously and unconsciously. If you typically find it easy to be authentic and show your true self but struggle to maintain authenticity and experience significant changes in your reactions, actions, thoughts, and emotions in the presence of a specific person, it is worthwhile to examine the dynamics of this relationship for signs of manipulation. Manipulation can occur in various contexts, including business relationships, as well as in family and friendship connections. This chapter focuses specifically on manipulation in intimate partnerships and close familial bonds.

Example:

Living authentically and following her inner truth is of utmost importance to Kathrine. However, she faces significant challenges in main-

taining this authenticity within her family, particularly with her partner and two children. When she is in the presence of her partner, her perception of reality, daily life, and overall experience differs from when she is alone. As a highly sensitive and empathetic individual, Kathrine keenly senses even the slightest emotional shifts in her partner, which in turn affect her own emotions. While she has learned to manage this sensitivity and create healthy boundaries, the pervasive atmosphere of her often-depressive partner strongly impacts her own mindset. As a result, Kathrine frequently feels disconnected from herself and her genuine emotions, making it difficult for her to engage in authentic conversations. When she shares her thoughts and perceptions with her partner, he responds with critical observations and maintains his own convictions, leaving her feeling invalidated:

- *"You're simply implying that. The truth is..."*
- *"That's nonsense. You're completely missing the point."*
- *"In reality, it's about..."*
- *"Just wait and see. I'm right."*
- *"Is that really the way you want to handle it?"*
- *"Everything will be fine..."*
- *"You're not doing it correctly."*

Kathrine holds her partner's opinion in high regard. However, his way of speaking consistently undermines her competence. Increasingly, she feels small and inadequate in his presence, causing her to constantly question her own views and feel swayed by his perspective. Even when she was previously confident in a decision, doubts arise as soon as she considers her partner's point of view.

Kathrine's children are perceptive of her insecure attitude, and they exploit her wavering nature more and more. They manipulate her by

112

knowing which arguments will make her change her mind, ultimately getting what they want but not necessarily what they need. Deep down, her children long for a mother who is internally clear and authentic, someone who knows her own desires and takes the lead in the relationship. Unfortunately, due to the repeated humiliation from her partner regarding her competence, Kathrine struggles to communicate her boundaries clearly and becomes increasingly intangible.

Within her partnership, Kathrine's old childhood wounds resurface. Any ideas, wishes, or new skills she wanted to bring into the family were often met with rejection or discouraged by her parents. They questioned her ability to make sound decisions and discouraged her from fully embracing her personality and actively influencing family dynamics. This eroded her self-esteem and self-confidence. She learned to constantly doubt herself, searching for faults within and deferring to others' opinions as the authority on what is right.

Unconsciously, her partner's behavior triggers memories of these old wounds, causing Kathrine to revert to familiar patterns of helplessness and powerlessness. This disconnects her from recognizing her true limits. In reality, Kathrine is fully aware of how she envisions her role as a mother and partner and which aspects of daily life hold significance for her. However, because she has learned that prioritizing others' needs over her own is necessary to maintain the family unit, it opens the door for manipulation, even if neither she nor her partner consciously intends it.

It can be beneficial for Kathrine to consistently create distance and prioritize time for herself. This time can be used to reconnect with her inner self and reflect on the following questions:

- *When do I genuinely feel like my authentic self?*
- *How does it feel to make decisions based on my intuition and inner coherence?*
- *What boundaries would I establish if there were no negative consequences in the relationship, such as withdrawal of love, anger, or bad mood?*
- *What do I truly desire? What kind of communication is necessary? How can I effectively counteract manipulation?*
- *Which individuals do I want to spend more time with, those with whom I effortlessly feel connected? Who are the people that mirror my true self?*

During this period of self-reflection, Kathrine has the opportunity to discover how she can authentically integrate her true personality into family life and establish clear boundaries with her partner. This process begins with reconnecting with herself.

Kathrine should determine the appropriate point at which she needs to assert her boundaries more firmly and create distance from her partner. While there is no one-size-fits-all solution, a general guideline is that if her partner respects her boundaries and actively works on improving his communication, there is potential for the relationship to thrive. However, if Kathrine consistently experiences negative reactions such as love withdrawal, disrespect, and a persistent bad mood from her partner whenever she expresses her authentic self and sets boundaries, she must consider whether this relationship truly supports her healing and personal growth or if it continuously reopens old wounds without genuine prospects for change. Regardless of the outcome, it is crucial for Kathrine to prioritize her own boundaries and cultivate authentic expression and clarity within her family dynamics. By doing so, she can regain a sense of leadership with her children, rebuild trust in herself and her perceptions, and create an environment that fosters her well-being and personal development.

People who consciously or unconsciously manipulate others often harbor deep insecurities and lack self-esteem and self-confidence. They believe they must manipulate others to fulfill their needs because they feel unsupported or inadequate. While manipulation can range from harmless to harmful, it is crucial for you to assert yourself clearly and reclaim responsibility for your own needs when faced with manipulation. If you sense that you are being manipulated, be mindful of a common trap: You might perceive the manipulator's neediness and feel emotionally obligated to be there for them to alleviate their pain. This can lead to neglecting your own well-being and struggling to establish boundaries. It requires courage to choose to say no and recognize that you are not responsible for fixing other people's problems. When you feel manipulated, seeking the perspective of someone outside the situation can be beneficial. By discussing the situation with a trusted outsider, you gain a fresh perspective and regain clarity. This process allows you to create emotional distance and examine the situation more objectively.

Inspiration

You should only engage in this exercise on days when you feel connected and grounded within yourself.

Find a comfortable place to sit and take a few deep breaths to center yourself.

Now, visualize thin threads attached to your body. These threads can be manipulated by others, influencing your actions and making you do things you didn't initiate yourself. If there is a specific situation in your life where you feel manipulated, imagine that the person involved is pulling these strings.

Next, release one of your hands and imagine holding a pair of large scissors. If you're feeling hopeless and weak, envision these scissors as magical, empowering tools. Use the scissors to cut all the threads connected to your body. Observe as the person manipulating you tries to hold onto the ends of the threads but is ultimately forced to let go. Remove any remaining remnants of the threads from your body and give yourself a good shake, symbolizing the release of their influence.

Take a deep breath and say aloud: "I am free. I have the freedom to move independently, choosing when, how, and where I want. No one can control me from the outside without my consent."

Affirmations

Here are some affirmations that can inspire you to embrace your boundaries and accept and respect them in everyday life:

I am a human being like everyone else. Therefore, I have the right to set boundaries like everyone else around me.

The right to personal boundaries is not something I have to earn. They arise from my pure existence and make me a human being in my being in the first place.

I have the right to live in an environment that respects my boundaries.

I am able to learn to communicate my boundaries in a way that is heard and accepted.

What I didn't learn as a child, I can always make up for.

I am an adult now. Unlike back then, I am now allowed to draw consequences if my boundaries are not respected.

I get to choose my relationships.

I am not forced to stay where I am.

I only have to be accountable to myself.

I decide for myself what I want to take responsibility for - and make wise choices in it.

I am willing to face the consequences of my own behavior and learn from it.

I am more than my tasks and obligations. I am more than a project. I am more than everyday life.

I have the right to quality of life. I am allowed to create this quality according to my own needs. I am wise enough and able to take into account in a healthy way the needs of the people for whom I am responsible.

I am allowed to say no. Every no to the outside is a yes to me and my way.

Boundaries protect what I hold most dear. Therefore, it is my job to set them up. The responsibility is mine.

When I set boundaries that show me authentically, I attract people into my life who are interested in my true nature. Those who turn away from me as soon as I become authentic do not belong to me.

I am allowed to feel everything that lives inside me. I have the right to cry, to mourn, to be angry, to feel helpless and powerless. These feelings are as sacred to me as my joy, enthusiasm, inspiration, and peace.

I am able to work through breakups and pain if needed after setting boundaries. I arrive more in my life through this and can heal and start anew.

My boundaries don't have to remain rigid. I'm allowed to change, and it's okay if not everyone agrees.

I am willing to make friends with people who can also set good boundaries themselves. In the long run, this does our friendship good. If I feel rejected by a boundary of the other person, I take responsibility for it and go into self-reflection and/or conversation.

I am not powerless in creating relationships at eye level. My views and approaches are allowed to influence every relationship I enter into.

I take responsibility for who I allow to influence me. What I learn, what interests me, and how I lead my life is up to me.

My boundaries may also have arisen from old experiences and serve me until I feel from within myself the need to grow beyond them. I do not have to force myself to eliminate old wounds as quickly as possible, but I may integrate them by paying special attention to my limits here.

I am aware that the topic of boundaries can regularly cause conflicts. I am prepared to decide which conflicts I would like to carry out, endure, and resolve and at which points I would rather say goodbye.

My goal is to grow from these processes. I believe that I can be strong and confident and leave a good, lasting impression in my life. My boundaries help me to do this.

Chapter 7

When Cinderella Set Boundaries – A Story of Self-Love

"However, bear in mind that every human power has its limits. How many objects are you able to grasp in such a way that they can be recreated through you? Reflect upon this, step beyond the familiar, and expand yourself as far as you can throughout the world."

Johann Wolfgang von Goethe

Once upon a time, there was a young woman who was called Cinderella by her family. Her real name was Ella, but no one cared about that. Cinderella's father had remarried, and her stepmother despised her. Something about Cinderella drove her stepmother to a boiling point. Was it Cinderella's graceful and subtle nature that accentuated her own rudeness? Was it that Cinderella, as the daughter of her stepmother's husband, had natural rights to the house and inheritance? Nothing was said about it.

The stepmother had brought her two daughters into the marriage, and they shared their mother's rejection of Cinderella. They mistreated and insulted their stepsister whenever they could. Even when Cinderella gave up her beautiful gabled room for the newcomers and moved into the small guest room, things didn't improve. Instead, the stepmother and her daughters took over the house, courtyard, and the servants. With domineering and crude attitudes, they commanded Cinderella without restraint:

"Clean my room!"

"Do my hair!"

"Make my bed!"

"Cook the food!"

Cinderella wished for the happiness of the three new family members. She tried to empathize with her stepsisters, who had left their home to join their mother in a new one after the marriage. She thought about her stepmother, who had left her whole life behind to be with Cinderella's father. So she convinced herself that if she were just neat and obedient, forgiving the hurtful comments and rude behavior, the new family members would eventually feel comfortable and change their attitude.

Day after day, Cinderella worked hard to please them. She cleaned, ironed, washed, cooked, and remained silent. She forgot all the things that used to bring her joy in everyday life, like singing and whistling—activities deemed too loud by her stepmother. She loved wearing dresses she made herself and dancing in them, but her stepsisters forbade it, taking up all the space to showcase themselves. She used to enjoy playing, laughing, and talking with the house animals and the servants, but now Cinderella toiled from morning till late at night.

As weeks turned into months, a deep heaviness settled over Cinderella's once cheerful and amiable spirit. Hardly anyone called her by her real name, Ella, anymore. She rarely had time for herself, unable to recall what brought her joy and gave her the courage to live her own life. She wondered what happened to the good times she had with her father. "Why doesn't he protect me?" she secretly asked herself. "He used to be so kind to me, but now he hardly cares. You're an adult now, Cinderella," he had told her some time ago. "Don't complain to me. If something bothers you, take care of it yourself."

Cinderella felt deeply hurt and sad, but she didn't want to show it because she was ashamed of her feelings. Instead, she buried them beneath her ceaseless busyness.

One day, a letter arrived in the mailbox—an invitation from the royal court. A ball was to be held in honor of the prince, who was seeking a wife. The two stepsisters chattered and cackled, claiming to be the new princess. They started pulling each other's hair and pushing each other around. Cinderella stood in the doorway, silently reading the invitation over and over again, as if in a daze. At that moment, a strong surge of anger and rage welled up within her. How could the prince decide who to marry without considering the woman's thoughts? How could Cinderella, who was no longer called Ella, let everything change so much and suppress how deeply she felt about it all?

In anger, she crumpled up the invitation, threw it on the floor, and ran outside. The stepsisters paused and watched her, confused.

Cinderella ran into the forest, crying. She found solace in a deep thicket on the edge of a clearing, where she sat on a tree stump and wept bitterly. Fear, helplessness, anger, and shame waged a battle within her. She no longer recognized herself and longed for her father to come and rescue her from the turmoil.

Suddenly, Cinderella heard a sound. Something moved in the middle of the clearing. A beam of light illuminated the area, and out of nowhere, a small, chubby, smiling old lady appeared before her.

Cinderella was astonished, her tears momentarily forgotten as she watched the little old lady approach.

"My child," she sang, "you called for me! Here I am. What can I do for you?"

Cinderella didn't understand. "I called for you?" she asked. "I didn't call anyone."

"Yes, you did," said the old lady. "You were crying out of anger and helplessness. So I came to speak with you. I am like the little helper who emerges from the heart when someone feels stuck, unable to move forward or backward. What is troubling you?"

Cinderella hesitated but eventually shared her concerns about the changes at home and her sadness over how everything had transformed, including herself. She cried about how poorly her family treated her, the loss of closeness with her father, who had always protected and loved her, and her life reduced to that of a mere servant.

"I miss living," she softly concluded. "I no longer know my purpose. I'm just a doormat for everyone in the neighborhood. I wanted to put on a brave face, but I can't anymore. And to make matters worse, the prince has invited me to the bridal ball, making me wonder if I'm destined to live solely for others and their supposed happiness. What about me? I feel so ashamed. I used to be so well-behaved and good. Now I'm asking these questions."

The old lady took a deep, smiling breath and gently placed her small, wrinkled hand on Cinderella's forearm. "Ella," she said, " Your feelings are trying to guide you. You've realized that something is wrong with what you're experiencing. The past is no more. Your world has changed. You were well-behaved and good because there was nothing to challenge it. You were taken care of and contented. But now you find yourself in a life that doesn't suit you. You are your father's daughter, with rights to the house and inheritance, the mistress of his heart, his only child. Yet, to please others, you behave like a servant seeking validation, not even deserving a kind word. What do you say to that? I know you wanted the best. But you're angry because you feel unappreciated in your service and have failed to fulfill your goal of ensuring a smooth transition for your new family members. You're ruining something beautiful with your ugly behavior."

Silently, Ella observed a small column of ants scurrying toward a large anthill. After what felt like an eternity, she shrugged her shoulders. "And now? What am I supposed to do? There seems to be no way out. In a minute, I'll return home, and my stepmother will scold me for being gone for so long. Then I'll have to dress up my two stepsisters and accompany them to the ball to sort peas all day. Do I have any other choice?"

Just then, Ella noticed a mischievous twinkle in the old woman's eyes. "Yes, Ella. There is another choice. It might be unfamiliar to you, but you need to reintroduce a word into your life. You didn't need it before your stepmother came along, but now it's crucial. The little word you need is 'no.'"

"No?!" Ella's eyes widened. "But... how can I simply say no? What will happen to all the work at home then? Stepmother will be furious! And Father... she'll surely tell him! And the sisters... let's not even think about it! No, we can't do that."

"You have already said no, dear Ella," the old woman gently replied. "But that 'no' is directed at yourself. It's always there.

Every time you say yes and go along with things, the 'no' is on the other side. When you mop the floor for the fifth time, even though your friends are waiting for you outside, you're saying yes to their demands and no to yourself. When you style your sisters' hair and deny yourself any enjoyment, you're saying yes to their maliciousness and no to yourself. When you remain silent and obedient in the face of their meanness, you're saying yes to the mistreatment and no to yourself. It's time for you to intervene, Ella. Yes, you! Don't wait for your father. Don't wait for people who don't share your desires to change their behavior. Don't wait for a prince to come and rescue you as the only way out, even if it's not what you truly want. Stop waiting for things to magically improve on their own. You have to take action. It's your life. Stand up and say no."

Ella was thunderstruck. She was supposed to act on her own? Was she expected to bid farewell to the part of herself that was good, sweet, well-behaved, and compliant? Was she meant to rise up and follow her anger? How was that even possible?

"But if I say no, I'll feel terrible! I still want to be a good person."

"Ella, you are a good person to someone who doesn't appreciate and value you. Look, I understand that this new message is challenging to grasp. It feels wrong because you're not accustomed to it. Let me give you something that can help."

The old woman reached into the wide folds of her skirt and revealed a leather pouch. She held it out to Ella, nodding in its direction. "Courage, my child," she cheerfully said, winking. "Reach inside! You'll feel various objects. Find the one that resonates with you."

With hesitance, Ella extended her hand and delved into the bag. She could feel different materials and shapes. Eventually, she encountered something soft, like cloth, between her fingers. She pulled it out.

The cloth exhibited several colors that shifted and intertwined as if moved by magic. The hues flowed into one another, constantly changing. Ella could hardly believe her eyes. After holding the cloth for a few seconds, it suddenly turned blue.

"A wise choice!" the old woman laughed, clapping her hands in delight. "This cloth speaks to you through its language of colors, revealing your true emotions. It wants to assist you in mindfully listening to your genuine feelings and ceasing to deceive yourself. It is the cloth of self-love."

"Self-love?" Ella shook her head. "I thought we were supposed to love others."

"That's correct, my dear. We are indeed meant to love others. But how can you love someone when the cloth turns black, indicating feelings of dislike, anger, powerlessness, and rage within you? How can you give love to others if it doesn't first ignite within yourself?"

"Hm..." Ella pondered, uncertain of how to counter that argument. She nodded and continued to examine the cloth thoughtfully.

"And how do I know how to interpret the colors?" she asked.

"You already understand the meaning of the color black. Currently, the cloth is blue, signifying hope in your heart."

"But I feel so down. How can there be hope?"

"You ran into the forest because deep down, you are searching for a way out. Since our encounter, hope for a positive outcome has been stirring within you. If you had already given up, you wouldn't be here at all. You would have retreated to your room and, within five minutes, resigned yourself to your duties. This cloth reveals what lies beneath surface-level emotions. How you interpret it is up to you. You can acknowledge what is happening but still choose to face the 'no.' Alternatively, you can decide to embrace your genuine feelings with a 'yes' and say 'no' to everything that no longer serves you. Remember, you can't love others until you have love within yourself to share."

Ella nodded. Although these ideas were new to her, they seemed plausible.

Before bidding farewell, the old woman explained the meanings of the other colors. "Go in peace, Ella. Seek peace within yourself. I wish you all the best."

"Goodbye," Ella replied. "Thank you very much!"

A flash of lightning illuminated the area, and the old woman vanished.

With the cloth in her hand, Ella stood in the clearing for a long time, gazing up at the sky. Then, she turned and made her way back home.

The next morning, Ella's stepmother's shrill voice echoed through the stone corridors. "Cinderella, come down immediately! My breakfast isn't ready! Will you, lazy girl, get out of bed?"

Ella sat on the edge of her bed and took a deep breath. She held the cloth in her hand and observed it. It was half black and half yellow—joy and anger. "I wonder what that means," she thought.

Well, I'm glad, Ella reflected, that I have an alternative to conforming to their demands. And I'm angry that I have to assert myself so strongly while others don't do the same.

The cloth gradually turned red. "I'm also afraid," Ella continued to think. "What will happen if I say no now?" The cloth slowly transitioned to blue. "Hope," Ella acknowledged. "This cloth has come to me for a reason. I won't let it be in vain. I'll give it a try."

Ella got dressed and descended the stairs. Upon reaching the kitchen door, she took a deep breath and entered.

"Good morning, Mother," she said calmly. "I apologize that your breakfast isn't ready yet. Unfortunately, I won't be able to prepare it as I have to leave right away. I've received an invitation, and I don't want to be late."

For a few seconds, the room fell into complete silence. Ella exhaled, and in that very moment, her stepmother rose from her seat, her face flushed, her eyes gleaming with malice, and her hands trembling. "You can't do it?" she dangerously whispered between clenched teeth. "You can't do it?" Then she burst into laughter. "Don't make me laugh, Cinderella. Go ahead, get to work!"

"No," Cinderella replied firmly. "I have to leave now. Goodbye, Mother." She turned and walked out. The door closed behind her. Ella strolled down the path toward her father's estate and waved to her friends who were already waiting for her. Together, they proceeded toward the village, singing and filled with joy.

*

This story tells the tale of a young woman we recognize from fairy tales as Cinderella. Traditionally, she is depicted as a well-mannered, beautiful, and graceful girl who escapes a cruel environment through her quiet and passive demeanor, ultimately finding salvation with the help of a fairy godmother. However, we are left unaware of what transpires in the castle and the outcome of her marriage with the prince—perhaps intentionally so.

Yet, our Cinderella, known as Ella in this account, has discovered that she is more than a damsel in distress who requires rescue. She delves deep within herself and confronts her inner world. Ella embraces the true beauty of her character—the range of her emotions and needs, her yearning for self-determination, and her own aspirations and dreams. She grants herself the permission to say no.

Ella has come to understand a crucial distinction between healthy adaptability ("I am a kind person, after all!") within a nurturing environment (such as the time she spent with her father and friends) and a harmful submission to an environment that brings her distress. She now recognizes that she can, and should, establish boundaries. Whether she continues to reside within her current surroundings will depend on how her family members choose to behave and whether they will honor Ella's boundaries.

Conclusion

"And humans have their limits!
Limits beyond which
Courage writhes in the dust,
The eye of wisdom goes blind,
Strength crumbles like reeds,
And the inner self timidly proclaims:
Thus far and no further!"

Franz Grillparzer

Isn't it wonderful that we can continuously experience, express, discover, and evolve through our boundaries? They provide the support we need, guide us to our inner truth, lead us towards self-love, enable deep connections with others, and reveal our true selves and desires.

Many of our boundaries don't require rebuilding; they simply require embracing and accepting them. How often do we struggle, believing that we have to be someone we're not deep inside? How much do we strive to conform, adjust, and contort to avoid feeling our pain? And how much happiness do we experience when our limits are acknowledged, respected, and even cherished? Our soul rejoices, and we cheer inside because we are finally seen!

It is an incredible gift to offer ourselves this wonderful experience first and foremost. It is never too late. Whenever we begin to love ourselves, it immediately changes our future.

Setting boundaries means saying yes to life—our life, your life. It means embracing our deep longing to live beyond mere survival and societal expectations. Saying no establishes an inner stance that says, "I am worthy." And you are worthy because I value you enough to reveal my true self. It is an invitation for you to truly see me, even when I say no. And perhaps, in that, you may discover a little more about yourself.

Be courageous in setting your boundaries, be prepared to rise again and again, and view self-love as an ongoing process that evolves and adapts alongside everything else—just like you, nature, relationships, and history. You can't lose, but you can gain so much and learn about yourself.

Perhaps each new boundary gives rise to five more, and each no prompts new questions about yes. But that's how life—your life—unfolds.

Wishing you all the best.

Resources and Further Reading

Brach, T. (2004). *Radical Acceptance: Embracing Your Life with the Heart of a Buddha*. Bantam.

Brown, B. (2010). *The Gifts of Imperfection: Let Go of Who You Think You're Supposed to Be and Embrace Who You Are*. Hazelden Publishing.

Gottlieb, L. (2019). *Maybe You Should Talk to Someone: A Therapist, HER Therapist, and Our Lives Revealed*. Houghton Mifflin Harcourt.

Lerner, H. (2014). *The Dance of Anger: A Woman's Guide to Changing the Patterns of Intimate Relationships*. Harper Paperbacks.

McGraw, P. (2013). *Life Code: The New Rules for Winning in the Real World*. Bird Street Books.

Neff, K. D. (2011). *Self-Compassion: The Proven Power of Being Kind to Yourself*. William Morrow Paperbacks.

Niequist, S. (2016). *Present Over Perfect: Leaving Behind Frantic for a Simpler, More Soulful Way of Living*. Zondervan.

Orloff, J. (2011). *Emotional Freedom: Liberate Yourself from Negative Emotions and Transform Your Life*. Harmony.

Rosenberg, M. B. (2005). *Speak Peace in a World of Conflict: What You Say Next Will Change Your World.* Puddle Dancer Press.

Rosenberg, M. B. (2015). *Nonviolent Communication: A Language of Life.* Puddledancer Press.

Schwartz, R. C. (2008). *You Are the One You've Been Waiting For: Bringing Courageous Love to Intimate Relationships.* Woodland Heights.

Siegel, D. J. (2010). *Mindsight: The New Science of Personal Transformation.* Bantam.

Van der Kolk, B. A. (2015). *The Body Keeps the Score: Brain, Mind, and Body in the Healing of Trauma.* Penguin Books.

Williams, M., & Penman, D. (2011). *Mindfulness: An Eight-Week Plan for Finding Peace in a Frantic World.* Rodale Books.

Printed in Great Britain
by Amazon

41802737R00076